Darfur

Other Books in the Current Controversies Series

Darfur

Debra A. Miller, Book Editor

GREENHAVEN PRESS
A part of Gale, Cengage Learning

Detroit • New York • San Francisco • New Haven, Conn • Waterville, Maine • London

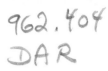

962.404
DAR

GALE
CENGAGE Learning

Christine Nasso, *Publisher*
Elizabeth Des Chenes, *Managing Editor*

© 2009 Greenhaven Press, a part of Gale, Cengage Learning

Gale and Greenhaven Press are registered trademarks used herein under license.

For more information, contact:
Greenhaven Press
27500 Drake Rd.
Farmington Hills, MI 48331-3535
Or you can visit our Internet site at gale.cengage.com

Articles in Greenhaven Press anthologies are often edited for length to meet page requirements. In addition, original titles of these works are changed to clearly present the main thesis and to explicitly indicate the author's opinion. Every effort is made to ensure that Greenhaven Press accurately reflects the original intent of the authors. Every effort has been made to trace the owners of copyrighted material.

Cover image copyright Issouf Sanogo/AFP/Getty Images.

LIBRARY OF CONGRESS CATALOGING-IN-PUBLICATION DATA

Darfur / Debra A. Miller, book editor.
     p. cm. -- (Current controversies)
   Includes bibliographical references and index.
   ISBN 978-0-7377-4456-9 (hardcover)
   ISBN 978-0-7377-4457-6 (pbk.)
   1. Sudan--History--Darfur Conflict, 2003- 2. Sudan--Politics and government-- 1985- 3. Genocide--Sudan--Darfur. 4. Darfur (Sudan)--Ethnic relations. 5. Ethnic conflict--Sudan--Darfur. I. Miller, Debra A.
   DT159.6.D27D3525 2009
   962.404'3--dc22
                                                                    2008055850

Printed in the United States of America
1 2 3 4 5 6 7 13 12 11 10 09

Contents

Monica Hill

The Darfur conflict originated in the colonial era when Britain administered northern and southern Sudan as separate colonies and favored the north; the neglect of southern Sudan continued after independence in the mid-1950s, sparking armed revolts against the government and leading to today's war in Darfur.

Stephan Faris

The violence in Darfur is usually attributed to ethnic divisions between Arabs and black rebel groups, but the conflict can be traced to the 1980s, when a severe drought caused by global warming pitted black farmers against Arab herders, initiating fighting between these groups over land and fueling a war that continues today.

Emily Wax

Although many commentators have emphasized the racial and ethnic aspects of the conflict in Darfur, the crisis there is really a political battle between Sudanese president Omar al-Bashir, who backs the Arab militia, and radical Islamic cleric Hassan al-Turabi, who is reportedly linked to one of Darfur's key rebel groups, the Justice and Equality Movement.

Chapter 2: Is the Sudanese Government Practicing Genocide?

Yes: The Sudanese Government Is Practicing Genocide

No: The Sudanese Government Is Not Practicing Genocide

Chapter 3: Is China Contributing to the Crisis in Darfur?

Yes: China Is Contributing to the Crisis in Darfur

Chapter 4: What Should Be Done to Bring Peace to Darfur?

Foreword

By definition, controversies are "discussions of questions in which opposing opinions clash" (Webster's Twentieth Century Dictionary Unabridged). Few would deny that controversies are a pervasive part of the human condition and exist on virtually every level of human enterprise. Controversies transpire between individuals and among groups, within nations and between nations. Controversies supply the grist necessary for progress by providing challenges and challengers to the status quo. They also create atmospheres where strife and warfare can flourish. A world without controversies would be a peaceful world; but it also would be, by and large, static and prosaic.

The Series' Purpose

The purpose of the Current Controversies series is to explore many of the social, political, and economic controversies dominating the national and international scenes today. Titles selected for inclusion in the series are highly focused and specific. For example, from the larger category of criminal justice, Current Controversies deals with specific topics such as police brutality, gun control, white collar crime, and others. The debates in Current Controversies also are presented in a useful, timeless fashion. Articles and book excerpts included in each title are selected if they contribute valuable, long-range ideas to the overall debate. And wherever possible, current information is enhanced with historical documents and other relevant materials. Thus, while individual titles are current in focus, every effort is made to ensure that they will not become quickly outdated. Books in the Current Controversies series will remain important resources for librarians, teachers, and students for many years.

In addition to keeping the titles focused and specific, great care is taken in the editorial format of each book in the series. Book introductions and chapter prefaces are offered to provide background material for readers. Chapters are organized around several key questions that are answered with diverse opinions representing all points on the political spectrum. Materials in each chapter include opinions in which authors clearly disagree as well as alternative opinions in which authors may agree on a broader issue but disagree on the possible solutions. In this way, the content of each volume in Current Controversies mirrors the mosaic of opinions encountered in society. Readers will quickly realize that there are many viable answers to these complex issues. By questioning each author's conclusions, students and casual readers can begin to develop the critical thinking skills so important to evaluating opinionated material.

Current Controversies is also ideal for controlled research. Each anthology in the series is composed of primary sources taken from a wide gamut of informational categories including periodicals, newspapers, books, U.S. and foreign government documents, and the publications of private and public organizations. Readers will find factual support for reports, debates, and research papers covering all areas of important issues. In addition, an annotated table of contents, an index, a book and periodical bibliography, and a list of organizations to contact are included in each book to expedite further research.

Perhaps more than ever before in history, people are confronted with diverse and contradictory information. During the Persian Gulf War, for example, the public was not only treated to minute-to-minute coverage of the war, it was also inundated with critiques of the coverage and countless analyses of the factors motivating U.S. involvement. Being able to sort through the plethora of opinions accompanying today's major issues, and to draw one's own conclusions, can be a complicated and frustrating struggle. It is the editors' hope that Current Controversies will help readers with this struggle.

Introduction

"Whatever name is given to the violence in Darfur, since 2003 it has caused the deaths of more than 300,000 people and displaced over 2 million others."

Darfur is a region in western Sudan, the largest country in Africa and a place where there are many cultural, racial, and religious divisions—between North African Arabs and sub-Saharan Africans, Muslims and Christians, nomads and farmers. Although intermarriage has blurred many of the physical differences among Sudan's population, the majority of people in Sudan's northern region are Arab Muslims with a nomadic history, while most southern Sudanese are non-Arab, black African farmers, many of whom practice traditional African religions or Christianity. Observers say the government, dominated by Arabs and based in the northern city of Khartoum, has long favored northern Arab tribes, often neglecting other parts of Sudan. Sudan's divisions have led to multiple conflicts in the country, including a decades-long civil war between the Sudanese government and rebels from southern Sudan and an ongoing conflict in Darfur.

Most commentators agree that the divisions in Sudan have been exacerbated by competition over resources. The discovery of oil in southern Sudan in 1978, for example, intensified the power struggle between northern Arabs and southern rebel groups. In addition, violence erupted in Darfur only after climate changes affected resources there. Historically, Arab nomads have migrated to fertile lands occupied by non-Arab farmers in Darfur during the dry season, and land disputes between the two groups have been resolved peacefully. Over the last few decades, however, the Darfur region experienced a prolonged drought that turned much of the land into desert, oil industry, and which reportedly sells arms to Sudan's government for use in Darfur—to force an end to the war in Darfur.

At this point, whether justice will ever be achieved and whether anyone will ever be punished for the atrocities committed in Darfur remains an open question, as does the ultimate fate of the people displaced from Darfur. The authors of the viewpoints included in *Current Controversies: Darfur* provide an array of opinions about the nature of the conflict in Darfur, whether it should be classified as genocide, whether China is contributing to the crisis, and what can or should be done at this juncture to finally bring peace to the region.

CHAPTER 1

What Is the Nature of the Crisis in Darfur?

Chapter Preface

During the past several years, despite a number of regional and United Nations' (UN) efforts to resolve the conflict in Darfur and protect the civilian population, violence continues to be a fact of life in the region and there has been little improvement in security. Only the dynamics of the conflict have changed, as new splinters appear among rebel groups, new alliances are formed, and people living in the Darfur region simply try to lie low and change their behaviors to avoid provoking attacks. During some months, these changed dynamics have produced a reduction in the number of attacks, but close observers say there have been no fundamental changes that will calm the crisis.

The establishment of a peacekeeping mission in 2004 (the African Union Mission in Sudan, or AMIS), for example, and the UN's augmenting of AMIS in 2006 to form the African Union/United Nations Hybrid Operation in Darfur, or UNAMID, is widely viewed as a failure. Many observers blame the obstructionist policies of the Sudanese government, and others criticize operational deficiencies, such as participating countries' slowness in providing equipment and deploying troops. Whatever the reason, UNAMID remains a weak force of peacekeepers that is subject to frequent attacks, is unable to protect Darfurians, and has failed to earn the trust of the local population.

Other actions by the UN have also so far been ineffective. Various resolutions—imposing an arms embargo, calling for an end to offensive military flights, demanding the disarmament of the goverment-back militia called the Janjaweed, and imposing sanctions such as a travel ban and asset freezes on individuals and companies—have not seemed to affect the violence on the ground. Similarly, the UN's 2005 referral of the Darfur matter to the International Criminal Court (ICC), and the court's subsequent indictment of several individuals for genocide, including Sudanese president Omar al-Bashir, have not produced any change in the government's tactics in Darfur.

Instead, the conflict has become more complicated, with an increasing number of parties and groups. For example, the Sudan Liberation Army (SLA), one of the two main Darfur rebel groups, splintered into two separate ethnic/tribal groups that began to fight each other, both targeting civilians from the opposite tribe. The two groups are led by Abdul Wahid Mohamed al Nour, who is supported by the Fur ethnic group, and Minni Arku Minawi, who draws support mainly from the Zaghawa tribe. The government's signing of a peace agreement in 2006 with Minni Minawi's SLA faction added to the violence, because it led the nonsignatory Fur rebel group led by Abdul Wahid Mohamed al Nour to escalate its attacks.

Another type of splintering is reportedly occurring within the Arab community. Although some Arabs in Darfur are still joining armed militias supported by the government, other Arab communities have sought to remain neutral. Still other Arabs actively oppose the government and have joined Darfur's rebel groups, and some have even formed their own antigovernment groups that attack and kidnap Sudanese soldiers. Recently, there also has been fighting among Arab tribes that make up much of Sudan's military forces.

Meanwhile, there are increased skirmishes across the border between Sudan and neighboring Chad. Insurgents trying to overthrow Chad's president Idriss Déby operate from Darfur, and some Sudanese rebels launch attacks into Sudan from bases in Chad. Efforts to police the border have broken down and the United Nations has sent a peacekeeping force into Chad, but the most recent reports are that the continuing unrest in eastern Chad is thwarting the efforts of humanitarian groups to come to the aid of hundreds of thousands of people who are living in refugee camps in Chad. The refugees include not only Chadians affected by rebel fighting but also people who fled from the massacre in Darfur.

The Sudanese government's response to the ongoing Darfur conflict has changed little over recent years. President Omar al-Bashir's administration continues to deny allegations that the government is participating in attacks on civilians. Instead, the government claims the violence is the result of agitation by rebel groups and battles between Darfur's various tribes over scarce resources. The government maintains it cannot negotiate effectively with rebels in Darfur because they are split into several disunited groups that have differing demands.

The stalemate in the Darfur conflict is now triggering threats of new violence from rebels. In 2008, representatives from the Justice and Equality Movement (JEM), one of the two original rebel groups from Darfur, said that if peace negotiations did not begin soon, the group would consider further actions against the government, including attacks geared towards removing the regime of al-Bashir.

As a result of the ICC's indictment of President al-Bashir for genocide in July 2008, the situation in Darfur has become even more unstable. The government flatly denied the allegations and warned that the charges could threaten its protection of humanitarian aid workers and peacekeepers, causing UNAMID to announce the evacuation of all nonessential personnel. The various causes and aspects of the Darfur conflict are the subject of the viewpoints in this chapter.

The Darfur Crisis Stems from Early Colonial Policies

Monica Hill

Monica Hill is a political journalist from the Atlanta area.

A few years ago, what people in the U.S. knew about Sudan, the largest country in Africa, likely came from the movie *Lawrence of Arabia*. Most had never heard of Darfur, the suffering, tumultuous region in western Sudan.

Darfuris are straining against predatory world imperialism and a repressive central government, which have together created a deadly civil war.

Today, Darfuris are caught in a grim conflict that has killed up to 400,000 people and displaced at least 2.5 million. The U.S. press and politicians are obscuring the historical roots of the agony, trying to manipulate public opinion about how to help. Shouts for a military solution dominate the airwaves, while providing aid for the hungry is not mentioned.

Darfur's conflict . . . goes back to the colonial era when Britain administered northern and southern Sudan as separate colonies.

Fundamentally, Darfuris are straining against predatory world imperialism and a repressive central government, which have together created a deadly civil war. An inexorable expansion of the Sahara Desert intensifies the suffering. The scope of the dilemma begs for revolutionary answers.

Monica Hill, "Tragedy in Darfur: Unraveling the Real Causes," *Freedom Socialist*, December 2006–January 2007, vol. 27. Reproduced by permission.

Colonial Legacy Breeds Civil War

Darfur's conflict today is an extension of Sudan's war between the north and south, Africa's longest civil war. Its origin goes back to the colonial era when Britain administered northern and southern Sudan as separate colonies.

After independence ..., the central government reinforced British policies of segregation of the north ... and of neglect and vicious suppression of the east, west and south.

British capital went largely to northern Sudan, which enabled the Nile Valley to develop industrially. The rest of Sudan was left out, exploited and impoverished, the people trying to sustain themselves on modes of production like herding and farming that became less and less viable.

After independence in the mid-1950s, the central government reinforced British policies of segregation of the north from the rest of the country and of neglect and vicious suppression of the east, west and south. At various times rebel groups mounted protests and armed revolts against the government.

Just as in the south, the have-nots in Darfur are rebelling against poverty and discrimination by the central government in Khartoum.

The strongest defiance came from the south, from 1955 to 1972, and again from 1983 to 2005. Then the Islamic fundamentalist dictatorship of Omar Al-Bashir signed a peace agreement with one of the groups, the Sudan People's Liberation Movement, which joined the government. Along with the settlement came 10,000 U.N. [United Nations] "peace-keeping" troops—and a shift of the fighting to Darfur.

Race Is Not to Blame

With starts and stops, the war now raging in Darfur has been going on since 2001. Just as in the south, the have-nots in Darfur are rebelling against poverty and discrimination by the central government in [the capital city of] Khartoum. The government strategy is to fund vicious counterinsurgent mercenaries, drawn from nomad tribes and called *Janjawid*. Terrified, unarmed civilians are the bulk of their victims.

The White House and U.S. media persist in characterizing this war and its barbarities as "Arab" vs. "Black African." But this is simply not true. Such deliberate mischaracterization is being done to further demonize Arabs and Muslims and thereby aid the U.S. "war on terror," and to promote military intervention.

As Professor Mahmood Mamdani, director of African Studies at Columbia University [New York], points out in an article published in [Internet magazine] *Black Commentator*, "All parties involved in the Darfur conflict—whether they are referred to as 'Arab' or as 'African'—are equally indigenous and equally black. All are Muslims and all are local." The so-called Arabs of Darfur are Africans who speak Arabic. The real roots of combat are not racial or ethnic but political and economic.

Disappearing water and vanishing fertile land contribute to hardships and divisions in Darfur. Less rain is falling, droughts are becoming more common and severe, and global warming and overuse of the land are causing the Sahara Desert, at the northern edge of Darfur, to grow. This hurts both the nomadic herders of camels and cattle who predominate in northern Darfur and the farmers who predominate to the south. Tensions are exacerbated as the herders press southward to find new grasslands.

Underdeveloped industrially, Darfur has no jobs for displaced nomads and farmers. Too many men end up in local militias or the Sudanese army. The women and children and elders are left behind, defenseless against raids, rape and plunder. What they all need is sane and humane development, not more troops!

Why Doesn't Anyone Mention Oil?

In most discussions about the crisis, the subject of oil doesn't come up. But it is Sudan's largest export and the reason for U.S. "concern" for Darfur.

A consortium of Chinese and other companies finished an oil pipeline in 1999. Since then, oil has turned Sudan into one of the fastest growing economies in the world, although the wealth benefits only a select few. Sudan is the third largest producer of oil in Africa. It also has large deposits of natural gas, uranium and copper.

Alas, the U.S. has no access to these riches, because the Clinton administration branded Sudan a "terrorist state" and imposed a blockade, as well as bombing its only major pharmaceutical plant in 1998. The China National Petroleum Corporation holds the only oil leases in Darfur. The U.S. *wants* that oil. And it wants a foothold in this region so well situated to exert military and political power over the Middle East.

That's why the U.S. favors sending U.N. troops into Darfur—and why China and France, with already established oil claims, do not.

Hope for Darfur, but Not Through U.N. Troops

The White House, Democrat and Republican politicians, and their media have now turned their attention to the intense violence and misery in Darfur—several years after it actually began.

Last Sept. 17 [2006], a Global Day for Darfur, thousands demonstrated in New York. Their main call was not for aid, but for 20,000 U.N. troops. Most of them were concerned young students and anti-war activists, chanting "Out of Iraq, into Darfur." They are unaware that the Save Darfur campaign is organized and financed primarily by the right wing—evangelical and Zionist groups and NGOs [nongovernmental organizations] funded by the [nonprofit organization] National Endowment for Democracy. Rally leaders met with George W. Bush in the White House just before the event.

U.N. and NATO [North Atlantic Treaty Organization, an alliance of democratic nations in Europe and North America] troops are hired to do what the empires, especially the U.S., tell them to do. From Korea to Congo, Iraq, Yugoslavia, Somalia and Haiti, the assigned role of "peacekeeper" troops has been colonial occupation and suppression of rebellious peoples, while stolen wealth flows into imperialist hands. Most of the NATO-funded African Union troops currently in Darfur are sent by vicious regimes that have themselves condoned atrocities similar to those of the *Janjawid*. Support for either U.N. or NATO-backed African Union soldiers in Darfur is support only for more death and destruction.

Many analysts say there is no hope for Darfur. And under the rule of world capitalism, they have a point. The human, economic and environmental catastrophes besetting Darfur are an acute example of what plagues former colonies all over the world.

Just as the problem is international, so is the solution. Only through an exchange of material resources and technological skills between richer and poorer countries will regions like Darfur recover from their torment. But, under the system of production for profit, equitable exchange is excluded.

Here and now, support for Darfur must include demanding the end of sanctions against Sudan along with immediate humanitarian relief and development aid for projects like irrigation. Aid that comes from governments must be unconditional. And, if there is any possibility of forming committees of women, farmers, herders and workers to make decisions about aid distribution, this should be fought for.

But just as important as calling for emergency aid is organizing for international socialism. This can be the only real foundation for a stunning recuperation by human beings and nature, in Darfur and beyond.

Global Warming Is the Root of the Problem in Darfur

Stephan Faris

Stephan Faris is a freelance journalist who writes from Africa and the Middle East. His is also the author of Forecast: The Consequences of Climate Change, from the Amazon to the Arctic, from Darfur to Napa Valley.

To truly understand the crisis in Darfur—and it has been profoundly misunderstood—you need to look back to the mid-1980s, before the violence between African and Arab began to simmer. Alex de Waal, now a program director at the [nonprofit organization] Social Science Research Council, was there at that time, as a doctoral candidate doing anthropological fieldwork. Earlier this year, he told me a story that, he says, keeps coming back to him.

A Story About Darfur

De Waal was traveling through the dry scrub of Darfur, studying indigenous reactions to the drought that gripped the region. In a herders' camp near the desert's border, he met with a bedridden and nearly blind Arab sheikh named Hilal Abdalla, who said he was noticing things he had never seen before: Sand blew into fertile land, and the rare rain washed away alluvial soil. Farmers who had once hosted his tribe and his camels were now blocking their migration; the land could no longer support both herder and farmer. Many tribesmen had lost their stock and scratched at millet farming on marginal plots.

The God-given order was broken, the sheikh said, and he feared the future. "The way the world was set up since time immemorial was being disturbed," recalled de Waal. "And it was bewildering, depressing. And the consequences were terrible."

The fighting in Darfur is usually described as racially motivated, . . . but the fault lines have their origins in . . . settled farmers and nomadic herders fighting over failing lands.

In 2003, another scourge, now infamous, swept across Darfur. Janjaweed [pro-government militia] fighters in military uniforms, mounted on camels and horses, laid waste to the region. In a campaign of ethnic cleansing targeting Darfur's blacks, the armed militiamen raped women, burned houses, and tortured and killed men of fighting age. Through whole swaths of the region, they left only smoke curling into the sky.

At their head was a 6-foot-4 Arab with an athletic build and a commanding presence. In a conflict the United States would later call genocide, he topped the State Department's list of suspected war criminals. De Waal recognized him: His name was Musa Hilal, and he was the sheikh's son.

The name Darfur *means "Land of the Fur" (the largest single tribe of farmers in Darfur), but the vast region holds the tribal lands—the* dars—*of many tribes.*

Fighting Over Failing Lands

The fighting in Darfur is usually described as racially motivated, pitting mounted Arabs against black rebels and civilians. But the fault lines have their origins in another distinction, between settled farmers and nomadic herders fighting over failing lands. The aggression of the warlord Musa Hilal can be traced to the fears of his father, and to how climate change shattered a way of life.

Until the rains began to fail, the sheikh's people lived amicably with the settled farmers. The nomads were welcome passers-through, grazing their camels on the rocky hillsides that separated the fertile plots. The farmers would share their wells, and the herders would feed their stock on the leavings from the harvest. But with the drought, the farmers began to fence off their land—even fallow land—for fear it would be ruined by passing herds. A few tribes drifted elsewhere or took up farming, but the Arab herders stuck to their fraying livelihoods—nomadic herding was central to their cultural identity. (The distinction between "Arab" and "African" in Darfur is defined more by lifestyle than any physical difference: Arabs are generally herders, Africans typically farmers. The two groups are not racially distinct.)

In 2003, a rebellion began in Darfur—a reaction against Khartoum's neglect and political marginalization of the region.

The name *Darfur* means "Land of the Fur" (the largest single tribe of farmers in Darfur), but the vast region holds the tribal lands—the *dars*—of many tribes. In the late 1980s, landless and increasingly desperate Arabs began banding together to wrest their own *dar* from the black farmers. In 1987, they published a manifesto of racial superiority, and clashes broke out between Arabs and Fur. About 3,000 people, mostly Fur, were killed, and hundreds of villages and nomadic camps were burned before a peace agreement was signed in 1989. More fighting in the 1990s entrenched the divisions between Arabs and non-Arabs, pitting the Arab pastoralists against the Fur, Zaghawa, and Massaleit [farming tribes]. In these disputes, Sudan's central government, seated in [the capital city of] Khartoum, often supported the Arabs politically and sometimes provided arms.

In 2003, a rebellion began in Darfur—a reaction against Khartoum's neglect and political marginalization of the region. And while the rebels initially sought a pan-ethnic front, the schism between those who opposed the government and those who supported it broke largely on ethnic lines. Even so, the conflict was rooted more in land envy than in ethnic hatred. "Interestingly, most of the Arab tribes who have their own land rights did not join the government's fight," says David Mozersky, the [nongovernmental organization] International Crisis Group's project director for the Horn of Africa [a penisula where Sudan is situated].

The roots of the drying of Darfur . . . lay in changes to the global climate.

The Role of Climate Change

Why did Darfur's lands fail? For much of the 1980s and '90s, environmental degradation in Darfur and other parts of the Sahel (the semi-arid region just south of the Sahara) was blamed on the inhabitants. Dramatic declines in rainfall were attributed to mistreatment of the region's vegetation. Imprudent land use, it was argued, exposed more rock and sand, which absorb less sunlight than plants, instead reflecting it back toward space. This cooled the air near the surface, drawing clouds downward and reducing the chance of rain. "Africans were said to be doing it to themselves," says Isaac Held, a senior scientist at the National Oceanic and Atmospheric Administration.

But by the time of the Darfur conflict four years ago, scientists had identified another cause. Climate scientists fed historical sea-surface temperatures into a variety of computer models of atmospheric change. Given the particular pattern of ocean-temperature changes worldwide, the models strongly predicted a disruption in African monsoons. "This was not caused by people cutting trees or overgrazing," says [New

York] Columbia University's Alessandra Giannini, who led one of the analyses. The roots of the drying of Darfur, she and her colleagues had found, lay in changes to the global climate.

The extent to which those changes can be blamed on human activities remains an open question. Most scientists agree that greenhouse gases have warmed the tropical and southern oceans. But just how much artificial warming—as opposed to natural drifts in oceanic temperatures—contributed to the drought that struck Darfur is as debatable as the relationship between global warming and the destruction of New Orleans. "Nobody can say that Hurricane Katrina [in 2005] was definitely caused by climate change," says Peter Schwartz, the co-author of a 2003 Pentagon report on climate change and national security. "But we can say that climate change means more Katrinas. For any single storm, as with any single drought, it's difficult to say. But we can say we'll get more big storms and more severe droughts."

With countries across the region and around the world suffering similar pressures, some see Darfur as a canary in the coal mine, a foretaste of climate-driven political chaos. Environmental degradation "creates very dry tinder," says de Waal. "So if anyone wants to put a match to it, they can light it up." Combustion might be particularly likely in areas where the political or social geography is already fragile. "Climate change is likely to cause tension all over the world," says Idean Salehyan, a political scientist at the University of North Texas. Whether or not it sparks conflict, he says, depends on the strength, goodwill, and competence of local and national governments.

Getting at the Roots of the Darfur Problem

In Darfur itself, recognizing climate change as a player in the conflict means seeking a solution beyond a political treaty between the rebels and the government. "One can see a way of de-escalating the war," says de Waal. "But unless you get at the underlying roots, it'll just spring back." One goal of the internationally sponsored peace process is the eventual return of locals to their land. But what if there's no longer enough decent land to go around?

If [Darfur's] collapse was in some part caused by the emissions from our factories, power plants, and automobiles, we bear some responsibility for the dying.

To create a new status quo, one with the moral authority of the God-given order mourned by Musa Hilal's father, local leaders would have to put aside old agreements and carve out new ones. Lifestyles and agricultural practices would likely need to change to accommodate many tribes on more fragile land. Widespread investment and education would be necessary.

But with Khartoum uncooperative, creating the conditions conducive to these sorts of solutions would probably require not only forceful foreign intervention but also a long-term stay. Environmental degradation means the local authorities have little or no surplus to use for tribal buy-offs, land deals, or coalition building. And fighting makes it nearly impossible to rethink land ownership or management. "The first thing you've got to do is stop the carnage and allow moderates to come to the fore," says Thomas Homer-Dixon, a political scientist at the University of Toronto. Yet even once that happens, he admits, "these processes can take decades."

Among the implications arising from the ecological origin of the Darfur crisis, the most significant may be moral. If the region's collapse was in some part caused by the emissions from our factories, power plants, and automobiles, we bear some responsibility for the dying. "This changes us from the position of Good Samaritans—disinterested, uninvolved people who may feel a moral obligation—to a position where we, unconsciously and without malice, created the conditions that led to this crisis," says Michael Byers, a political scientist at the University of British Columbia. "We cannot stand by and look at it as a situation of discretionary involvement. We are already involved."

The Darfur Crisis Is Primarily a Political Conflict

Emily Wax

Emily Wax is a reporter for the Washington Post, *a daily national newspaper published in Washington, D.C.*

Heard all you need to know about Darfur? Think again. [Several] years after a government-backed militia began fighting rebels and residents in this region of western Sudan, much of the conventional wisdom surrounding the conflict— including the religious, ethnic and economic factors that drive it—fails to match the realities on the ground. Tens of thousands have died and some 2.5 million have been displaced, with no end to the conflict in sight. Here are five truths to challenge the most common misconceptions about Darfur:

Nearly Everyone Is Muslim

Early in the conflict, I was traveling through the desert expanses of rebel-held Darfur when, amid decapitated huts and dead livestock, our SUV roared up to an abandoned green and white mosque, riddled with bullets, its windows shattered.

Darfur is home to some of Sudan's most devout Muslims, in a country where 65 percent of the population practices Islam, the official state religion.

In my travels, I've seen destroyed mosques all over Darfur. The few men left in the villages shared the same story: As government Antonov jets dropped bombs, Janjaweed [pro-government] militia members rode in on horseback and attacked the town's mosque—usually the largest structure in town. The strange thing, they said, was that the attackers were Muslim, too. Darfur is home to some of Sudan's most devout Muslims, in a country where 65 percent of the population practices Islam, the official state religion.

A long-running but recently pacified war between Sudan's north and south did have religious undertones, with the Islamic Arab-dominated government fighting southern Christian and animist African rebels over political power, oil and, in part, religion.

"But it's totally different in Darfur," said Mathina Mydin, a Malaysian nurse who worked in a clinic on the outskirts of Nyala, the capital of South Darfur. "As a Muslim myself, I wanted to bring the sides together under Islam. But I quickly realized this war had nothing to do with religion."

Although the conflict has also been framed as a battle between Arabs and black Africans, everyone in Darfur appears dark-skinned, at least by the usual American standards.

Everyone Is Black

Although the conflict has also been framed as a battle between Arabs and black Africans, everyone in Darfur appears dark-skinned, at least by the usual American standards. The true division in Darfur is between ethnic groups, split between herders and farmers. Each tribe gives itself the label of "African" or "Arab" based on what language its members speak and whether they work the soil or herd livestock. Also, if they attain a certain level of wealth, they call themselves Arab.

Sudan melds African and Arab identities. As Arabs began to dominate the government in the past century and gave jobs to members of Arab tribes, being Arab became a political advantage; some tribes adopted that label regardless of their ethnic affiliation. More recently, rebels have described themselves as Africans fighting an Arab government. Ethnic slurs used by both sides in recent atrocities have riven communities that once lived together and intermarried.

"Black Americans who come to Darfur always say, 'So where are the Arabs? Why do all these people look black?'" said Mahjoub Mohamed Saleh, editor of Sudan's independent Al-Ayam newspaper. "The bottom line is that tribes have intermarried forever in Darfur. Men even have one so-called Arab wife and one so-called African. Tribes started labeling themselves this way several decades ago for political reasons. Who knows what the real bloodlines are in Darfur?"

Although analysts have emphasized the racial and ethnic aspects . . . , a long-running political battle between Sudanese President Omar Hassan Bashir and radical Islamic cleric Hassan al-Turabi may be more relevant.

It's All About Politics

Although analysts have emphasized the racial and ethnic aspects of the conflict in Darfur, a long-running political battle between Sudanese President Omar Hassan Bashir and radical Islamic cleric Hassan al-Turabi may be more relevant.

A charismatic college professor and former speaker of parliament, Turabi has long been one of Bashir's main political rivals and an influential figure in Sudan. He has been fingered as an extremist; before the Sept. 11, 2001, attacks [in the United States] Turabi often referred to Osama bin Laden as a hero. More recently, the United Nations [U.N.] and human rights experts have accused Turabi of backing one of Darfur's key rebel groups, the Justice and Equality Movement, in which some of his top former students are leaders.

Because of his clashes with Bashir, Turabi is usually under house arrest and holds forth in his spacious Khartoum villa for small crowds of followers and journalists. But diplomats say he still mentors rebels seeking to overthrow the government.

"Darfur is simply the battlefield for a power struggle over Khartoum," said Ghazi Suleiman, a Sudanese human rights lawyer. "That's why the government hit back so hard. They saw Turabi's hand, and they want to stay in control of Sudan at any cost."

China and Chad have played key roles in the Darfur conflict.

This Conflict Is International

China and Chad have played key roles in the Darfur conflict.

In 1990, Chad's [president] Idriss Deby came to power by launching a military blitzkrieg from Darfur and overthrowing President Hissan Habre. Deby hails from the elite Zaghawa tribe, which makes up one of the Darfur rebel groups trying to topple the government. So when the conflict broke out, Deby had to decide whether to support Sudan or his tribe. He eventually chose his tribe.

Now the Sudanese rebels have bases in Chad; I interviewed them in towns full of Darfurians who tried to escape the fighting. Meanwhile, Khartoum [the capital city of Sudan, and the seat of government] is accused of supporting Chad's anti-Deby rebels, who have a military camp in West Darfur. (Sudan's government denies the allegations.). . . [In 2006], bands of Chadian rebels nearly took over the capital, N'Djamena. When captured, some of the rebels were carrying Sudanese identification.

Meanwhile, Sudan is China's fourth-biggest supplier of imported oil, and that relationship carries benefits. China, which holds veto power in the U.N. Security Council [the United Nation's main decision-making body], has said it will stand by Sudan against U.S. efforts to slap sanctions on the country and in the battle to force Sudan to replace the African Union peacekeepers with a larger U.N. presence. China has built highways and factories in Khartoum, even erecting the Friendship Conference Hall, the city's largest public meeting place.

The "Genocide" Label Made It Worse

Many of the world's governments have drawn the line at labeling Darfur as genocide. Some call the conflict a case of ethnic cleansing, and others have described it as a government going too far in trying to put down a rebellion.

Rather than spurring greater international action, [the genocide] label only seems to have strengthened Sudan's rebels.

But in September 2004, [U.S.] then-Secretary of State Colin L. Powell referred to the conflict as a "genocide." Rather than spurring greater international action, that label only seems to have strengthened Sudan's rebels; they believe they don't need to negotiate with the government and think they will have U.S. support when they commit attacks. Peace talks have broken down seven times, partly because the rebel groups have walked out of negotiations. And Sudan's government has used the genocide label to market itself in the Middle East as another victim of America's anti-Arab and anti-Islamic policies.

Perhaps most counterproductive, the United States has failed to follow up with meaningful action. "The word 'genocide' was not an action word; it was a responsibility word," Charles R. Snyder, the State Department's senior representative on Sudan, told me in late 2004. "There was an ethical and moral obligation, and saying it underscored how seriously we took this." The Bush administration's recent idea of sending several hundred NATO [North Atlantic Treaty Organization, an alliance of democratic nations in Europe and North America] advisers to support African Union peacekeepers falls short of what many advocates had hoped for.

"We called it a genocide and then we wine and dine the architects of the conflict by working with them on counterterrorism and on peace in the south," said Ted Dagne, an Africa expert for the Congressional Research Service [a division of the Library of Congress that provides research to the U.S. Congress]. "I wish I knew a way to improve the situation there. But it's only getting worse."

The Conflict in Darfur Has Created a Catastrophic Humanitarian Crisis

Merle D. Kellerhals

Merle D. Kellerhals is a staff writer for the U.S. State Department's Bureau of International Information Programs.

The humanitarian crisis in the Darfur region of Sudan is worsening and the number of killed and displaced people continues to grow, reflecting an atmosphere of continuing violence, a senior U.S. diplomat says.

The Genocide Continues

"The conflict that has created all of this humanitarian suffering has mutated from the Sudanese government's counterinsurgency campaign against new active rebel groups in Darfur in 2003, which targeted innocent Darfurians with unconscionable savagery, to a situation that is complicated by shifting alliances, growing ambitions, tribal conflicts and regional meddling," says Ambassador Richard Williamson, the U.S. special envoy to Sudan.

"The government of Sudan, the Arab militias, and rebel leaders all have blood on their hands," he said. "Make no mistake: this 'genocide in slow motion' continues, casualties mount, and more must be done to alleviate the terrible humanitarian suffering and bring sustainable stability and peace to this region brutalized and stained with the blood of innocent people."

Williamson testified before the Senate Foreign Relations Committee April 23 [2008] that since 2003 an estimated 200,000 people have died in Darfur as a result of the con-

Merle D. Kellerhals, "Humanitarian Crisis in Darfur Worsening, U.S. Envoy Says," America.gov, April 24, 2008. U.S. Department of State, Washington, DC.

flict and some 2.5 million people have been displaced inside Darfur or into neighboring Chad.

The Senate Foreign Relations Committee convened an oversight hearing April 23 to determine what progress has been made since the United Nations and African Union assumed joint control of peacekeeping December 31, 2007, and to evaluate the U.S. response.

The Humanitarian Situation

Committee Chairman Joseph Biden said that violence and banditry are still common. "Last week, the World Food Programme announced that it is going to have to cut rations for people in Darfur in half because so many of its trucks are being hijacked that it cannot maintain supply lines," Biden said.

Darfur is the focus of the largest international humanitarian operation in the world.

Katherine Almquist, assistant administrator for Africa in the U.S. Agency for International Development [USAID, the U.S. government's agency that provides economic and humanitarian assistance worldwide], told the senators that after three years into the six-year road map known as the Comprehensive Peace Agreement, "comprehensive peace in Sudan remains elusive."

Sudan is USAID's largest program in Africa and among the largest in the world, she said. It remains the United States' top foreign policy priority in Africa, and Darfur is the focus of the largest international humanitarian operation in the world.

"This devastating conflict has left 2.5 million people internally displaced and another 250,000 refugees in Chad," she said. "Since 2004, USAID has spent an average of $750 million annually in assistance to Sudan, including a total of $1.5 billion in humanitarian assistance in Darfur and eastern Chad [over the same period]."

Peacekeeping Efforts

John Holmes, under-secretary-general for U.N. [United Nations] humanitarian affairs, told the U.N. Security Council April 22 [2008] in a special briefing that he was "saddened and angry" to inform the council that the situation inside Darfur had only worsened in the past 12 months. He advised the Security Council that the joint U.N.-African Union peacekeeping force would not reach full strength—26,000 peacekeepers and police officers—until 2009.

He said that to date only 9,000 peacekeepers have been sent into the Darfur region to replace a 7,000-strong African Union force.

In addition, the U.N.-African Union peacekeeping force representative, Rodolphe Adada, said the force lacks five critical elements to become fully operational—attack helicopters, surveillance aircraft, transport helicopters, military engineers and logistical support.

Williamson said that the government-supported Janjaweed militias that are responsible for most of the attacks on civilians have not been disarmed or controlled, as required in the Darfur Peace Agreement. But he noted that these were not the only groups responsible for violence and death in the region.

Despite initial cooperation, the Sudanese government has created new impediments that further hamper humanitarian programs.

The deployment of a joint U.N.-African Union peacekeeping mission would be a significant step toward improved security in Darfur, Williamson said. "But unfortunately, since the transition from the African Union Mission in Sudan to the

AU-U.N. peacekeeping operation, UNAMID, there has been little change on the ground," he said.

Almquist said that despite initial cooperation, the Sudanese government has created new impediments that further hamper humanitarian programs.

Williamson said the United States has contributed significant funding for peacekeeping, in addition to funding 25 percent of these missions through its peacekeeping dues to the United Nations. The United States contributed more than $450 million to construct and maintain 34 base camps in Darfur for peacekeepers.

In addition, the United States has committed more than $100 million to bolster African nations' will to step forward and provide peacekeepers for Darfur, he said.

Darfur Is a Place Where Torture Is Rampant

Physicians for Human Rights

Physicians for Human Rights is a nongovernmental group that mobilizes health professionals to investigate human rights abuses and advance health, dignity, and justice around the world.

One of the . . . presenters at the Amel Center [a program of the Sudan-based Amel Center for Treatment and Rehabilitation of Victims of Torture] training doctors to treat victims of torture, was [until 2007] their Director for Treatment, Dr. Mohamed Ahmed. He is also a 2007 recipient of the Robert F. Kennedy Memorial Award. The following is a [partial] transcript of Dr. Ahmed's remarks. . . .

Torture in Darfur's War

The purpose of torture is to humiliate the victim. Innocent civilians have come [to us] during course of battles, hit in course of attacks—some have been beaten up by different people either with ends of rifles, or with cables or wires. Some people were subjected to this. Some people have been severely burned; some have been referred to Amel in Khartoum [Sudan's capital city] to be treated. Others had bone problems, so they have been referred to orthopedic surgeons. Some have had severe psychological trauma. Some are unable to speak altogether—psychogenic consequences. My last patient was a female university student and as a result of the trauma, she was totally blind, and we had to refer her to a psychiatrist. In addition, people have cigarette burns on their bodies. All this has been documented.

This is dangerous and serious. Rebels and fighters have the arms. The civilians are innocent and this is our responsibility.

Susannah Sirkin, "Torture in Darfur," *Sudan Journal*, Physicians for Human Rights, 2007. Copyright © 2007 Physicians for Human Rights. Reproduced by permission.

We have to be one community, and we have to stand against this together. We are fully qualified professional people. If we don't address this as professionals, we will lose our society.

Some people are subjected to beating, men are whipped and given lashes, some are tortured at gunpoint.

Torture Is a Part of Daily Life

Another problem is what happens to people during their daily movements. Women are most victimized because they are assaulted in the course of their daily activities. In 2005, in the outskirts of camps, women have been attacked. Even in camps, they've been attacked. In one instance recently, more than eighteen women were gang raped. Eight or nine of these cases have been documented. The rapists fled the scene. Not only have they been raped, their genitalia have also been mutilated. They are also subjected to verbal abuse and assault. All of this is meant to degrade the dignity of the person.

Some people are subjected to beating, men are whipped and given lashes, some are tortured at gunpoint. Worse, some people are kidnapped, and no one knows what happened to them. Their families tell us they have "disappeared," and no one knows what happens. In the Kailek area, people have been subjected to sexual slavery. All of these are documented incidents. Some people are blindfolded, and they are taken to unknown locations and asked to carry cargo. Some have had their hands attached to their legs and then were hanged from trees, and some of them have been totally paralyzed as a result.

Torture in Detention Centers

I also want to talk about what has happened to people in detention centers—either at the hands of military intelligence, security forces, or police forces. Most people say that the best treatment they got was from police forces. There, they are usually deprived of food and water and maybe beaten, but military intelligence detainees are often tied up and lose consciousness, are given only one meal a day, and are held for many weeks. They can use the toilet only in morning and evening. If you see the detention centers, you will see there are more than twenty people held in 2 × 2 meter cells.

Recently people came from camps where people have been forced to drink their own urine. You cannot believe this if you don't meet the person. It causes diarrhea. Some other groups who have come from north Darfur were exposed to rape inside the detention center. Some people were forced to sit naked on chili or hot pepper. Sometimes the chili is burnt and you are put inside a very hot room. We had to transfer them for psychological treatment.

More than 90% [of the torture] has happened at the hand of Government of Sudan forces or Janjaweed forces.

The most serious cases involve citizens who are being forced into slavery. The humiliation is more painful than any physical punishment. The degradation and loss of dignity is the worst. When people are transferred from detention center to prison, the treatment may be less severe there, and food and other support is the most serious problem they have to deal with. Hunger is a major problem. There is limited capacity in the detention centers.

There are also underground prisons where people are placed in a hole in the ground under a zinc sheet. They are taken out at night and tortured and then returned to these underground prisons. Some people cannot even go to toilet except in evening. When they tried to flee, they were slaughtered. In one case, a government officer in charge stopped this. This is in the Sudan where we claim to be an Islamic state. More than 90% has happened at hand of Government of Sudan forces or Janjaweed forces. Some people have been detained and tortured by rebel forces.

Deep Social Ramifications

In one of my rounds, a woman came who had no physical symptoms. She was in state of severe depression. I started to talk to her and after some time I realized she was exposed to repeated rape. In the center, we could rehabilitate her socially, and she could marry and lead a normal life. However there are some people who could not make it. They had to leave Sudan because they have been rejected by the community. These are difficult questions that we have to answer. It is difficult to differentiate between psychological and physical treatment and how to reintegrate people into the society. Article 149 of Sudan's Criminal Code does not recognize rape unless there are four male witnesses. If the victim goes to a court of law, she will be punished as one who is sinful. This is a very difficult problem in a Muslim community. This has deep social ramifications.

Rape Is the Worst Problem in the Darfur War

Glenys Kinnock

Glenys Kinnock is a contributing writer for New Statesman.

Saida Abdukarim was eight months pregnant and tending her vegetables when she was raped and beaten by men who told her: "You are black, so we can rape you." As the blows rained down she crouched to protect her unborn baby. The baby is still alive. She, however, is unable to walk.

Her story, recorded by the journalist Nicholas Kristof, is not unique or even unusual. In Darfur, where close to 400,000 have died in a government-sponsored programme of ethnic cleansing, rape is a weapon used to break the will of communities, weaken tribal ties and humiliate people to the point where they abandon their land.

Every day women in Darfur risk rape and assault when they leave their homes . . . even though the international community claims it is protecting them.

Rape Is a Daily Occurence

Every day women in Darfur risk rape and assault when they leave their homes to find food or firewood—even though the international community claims it is protecting them. And if they survive an attack their prospects are still bleak. Many have seen their villages burned and their male relatives killed; they must walk for days to refugee camps, through baking heat and dust storms, carrying their children. Here, instead of

Glenys Kinnock, "The Victims of Mass Rape Need our Help," newstatesman.com, January 30, 2006. Reproduced by permission. http://www.newstatesman.com/200601300007.

finding safety and comfort, they must build their own shelters—and they are still vulnerable to attack.

No one knows how many women are raped because [Sudanese] society shames the victims into silence.

No one knows how many women are raped because their society shames the victims into silence. Until a few weeks ago, women who sought medical help after being raped were arrested by the Sudanese security forces. (The arrests stopped when the international community complained, proving we can make a difference when we bother.)

We haven't heard much about Darfur recently. The killing and raping continue, but the regime in Khartoum has changed tactics. It has achieved its racist aim: 90 per cent of the black African villages have been destroyed. So now it is using its proxies, the Janjaweed militia, to rape women whenever they venture out for firewood. The international community, it calculates, is not going to cause a fuss over the suffering of women who cannot bear to talk about their ordeal.

Is this what innocent women and children deserve? Is this the best we can do for them?

If we don't act now Darfur will have a generation of women who . . . must live with the stigma all their lives.

A Call to the International Community to Help

The United Nations has repeatedly refused to send peacekeepers to Darfur. However, there are other steps we can take. We could send policewomen from African nations to accompany the firewood-gathering trips—civilian police would not represent the challenge to Sudanese sovereignty that soldiers would. We could provide fuel-efficient stoves so less firewood is needed. We could vastly increase the number of African Union monitors, to deter the rapists. We could provide rape counselling and a chance to break the taboo of silence. We could increase treatment for sexually transmitted diseases.

If we don't act now Darfur will have a generation of women who are either unable to have children because of infection or physical damage or who have been raped and got pregnant and so must live with the stigma all their lives, unable to get married.

Action requires political will, and so far this has been lacking. But we must keep the pressure on. We must shame the UN [United Nations], the European Commission and our own governments into doing something. Kofi Annan described Darfur as "little short of hell on earth." It is time to end that hell, for Saida and the thousands like her.

Current
CONTROVERSIES

CHAPTER 2

Is the Sudanese Government Practicing Genocide?

Chapter Overview

Scott Straus

Scott Straus is an assistant professor of political science at the University of Wisconsin in Madison, Wisconsin.

In Sudan's western Darfur region, a massive campaign of ethnic violence has claimed the lives of more than 70,000 [now more than 300,000] civilians and uprooted an estimated 1.8 million [now more than 2 million] more since February 2003. The roots of the violence are complex and parts of the picture remain unclear. But several key facts are now well known. The primary perpetrators of the killings and expulsions are government-backed "Arab" militias. The main civilian victims are black "Africans" from three tribes. And the crisis is currently the worst humanitarian disaster on the planet.

Much of the public debate in the United States and elsewhere [about Darfur] ... has focused ... on whether or not it should be called a "genocide" under the terms of the Genocide Convention.

The bloodshed in Darfur has by now received a great deal of attention. Much of the public debate in the United States and elsewhere, however, has focused not on how to stop the crisis, but on whether or not it should be called a "genocide" under the terms of the Genocide Convention [a 1948 treaty that defines and prohibits genocide]. Such a designation, it was long thought, would inevitably trigger an international response. . . .

So far, the convention has proven weak. Having been invoked, it did not—contrary to expectations—electrify international efforts to intervene in Sudan. Instead, the UN [United Nations] Security Council [the main decision-making body of the United Nations] commissioned further studies and vaguely threatened economic sanctions against Sudan's growing oil industry if Khartoum [Sudan's capital and the seat of government] did not stop the violence; one council deadline has already passed without incident. Although some 670 African Union [a federation of African Nations] troops have been dispatched to the region with U.S. logistical assistance to monitor a nonexistent ceasefire, and humanitarian aid is pouring in, the death toll continues to rise. The lessons from Darfur, thus, are bleak. Despite a decade of handwringing over the failure to intervene in Rwanda [another country that experienced mass killings] in 1994 and despite Washington's decision to break its own taboo against the use of the word "genocide," the international community has once more proved slow and ineffective in responding to large-scale, state-supported killing. Darfur has shown that the energy spent fighting over whether to call the events there "genocide" was misplaced, overshadowing difficult but more important questions about how to craft an effective response to mass violence against civilians in Sudan. The task ahead is to do precisely that: to find a way to stop the killing, lest tens of thousands more die. . . .

Army forces and the militia often attack together, . . . [and] in some cases, government aircraft bomb areas before the militia attack.

The Violence in Darfur

Human rights groups, humanitarian agencies, and the U.S. State Department have all reached strikingly similar conclusions about the nature of the violence. Army forces and the militia often attack together, as janjaweed [government-backed militia not officially part of Sudan's armed forces] leaders readily admit. In some cases, government aircraft bomb areas before the militia attack, razing settlements and destroying villages; such tactics have become central to this war. In late September, a U.S. official reported that 574 villages had been destroyed and another 157 damaged since mid-2003. Satellite images show many areas in Darfur burned out or abandoned. The majority of the attacks have occurred in villages where the rebels did not have an armed presence; Khartoum's strategy seems to be to punish the rebels' presumed base of support—civilians—so as to prevent future rebel recruitment.

Testimony recorded at different times and locations consistently shows that the attackers single out men to kill. Women, children, and the elderly are not spared, however. Eyewitnesses report that the attackers sometimes murder children. For women, the primary threat is rape; sexual violence has been widespread in this conflict. Looting and the destruction of property have also been common after the janjaweed and their army allies swoop down on civilian settlements.

This violence has produced what one team of medical researchers has termed a "demographic catastrophe" in Darfur. By mid-October 2004, an estimated 1.8 million people—or about a third of Darfur's population—had been uprooted, with an estimated 1.6 million Darfurians having fled to other parts of Sudan and another 200,000 having crossed the border to Chad [a country bordering Sudan]. Exactly how many have died is difficult to determine; most press reports cite about 50,000, but the total number is probably much higher. In October 2004, a World Health Organization official estimated that 70,000 displaced persons had died in the previous six months from malnutrition and disease directly related to their displacement—a figure that did not include violent deaths. By now, the number has probably grown much larger. Despite a huge influx of humanitarian aid since mid-2004, the International Committee of the Red Cross warned in October of an "unprecedented" food crisis; several months earlier, a senior official with the U.S. Agency for International Development told journalists that the death toll could reach 350,000 by the end of the year [2005]. . . .

Word Play

Khartoum has, predictably, denied direct involvement in the attacks against civilians, and both the Arab League [political and economic federation of north Africa and the Middle Eastern countries] and the African Union have downplayed the gross violations of human rights. Still, not much controversy exists over what is actually happening in Darfur. Yet public debate in the United States and Europe has focused less on the violence itself than on what to call it—in particular, whether the term "genocide" applies.

The genocide debate took off in March 2004, after *New York Times* columnist Nicholas Kristof published a number of articles making the charge. His graphic depictions of events there soon stimulated similar calls for action from an unlikely combination of players—Jewish-American, African-American, liberal, and religious-conservative constituencies. . . .

Proponents of applying the "genocide" label . . . argued that . . . the violence targeted an ethnic group for destruction, was systematic and intentional, and was state supported.

Proponents of applying the "genocide" label emphasized two points. First, they argued that the events in Sudan met a general standard for genocide: the violence targeted an ethnic group for destruction, was systematic and intentional, and was state supported. Second, they claimed that under the Genocide Convention, using the term would trigger international intervention to halt the violence. Salih Booker and Ann-Louise Colgan from the advocacy group Africa Action wrote in *The*

Nation, "We should have learned from Rwanda that to stop genocide, Washington must first say the word."

Colgan and Booker made a fair point. During the Rwandan genocide—exactly a decade before Darfur erupted—State Department spokespersons in Washington were instructed not to utter the "g-word," since, as one internal government memorandum put it, publicly acknowledging "genocide" might commit the U.S. government to do something at a time when President Bill Clinton's White House was entirely unwilling. As a result, the United States and the rest of the world sat on the sidelines as an extermination campaign claimed at least half a million civilian lives in three months. In the aftermath, many pundits agreed that a critical first step toward a better response the next time would be to openly call a genocide "genocide."

The idea that states are obligated to do something in the face of genocide comes from two provisions in the Genocide Convention.

The idea that states are obligated to do something in the face of genocide comes from two provisions in the Genocide Convention. First, the treaty holds that contracting parties are required to "undertake to prevent and to punish" genocide. Second, Article VIII of the convention stipulates that signatories may call on the UN to "take such action . . . for the prevention and suppression" of genocide. Prior to the Darfur crisis, and in light of the way the genocide debate unfolded in Rwanda, the conventional wisdom was that signatories to the convention were obligated to act to prevent genocide if they recognized one to be occurring. The convention had never been tested, however, and the law is in fact ambiguous on what "undertaking to prevent" and "suppressing" genocide actually mean and who is to carry out such measures.

In July [2004], the U.S. House of Representatives entered the rhetorical fray by unanimously passing a resolution labeling the violence in Sudan "genocide." The resolution called on the [George W.] Bush administration to do the same and, citing the convention, to "seriously consider multilateral or even unilateral intervention to prevent genocide" if the UN Security Council failed to act. The Bush administration, however, interpreted its international obligations differently. Facing mounting appeals to call Darfur "genocide," [Secretary of State Colin] Powell insisted that such a determination, even if it came, would not change U.S. policy toward Sudan. Powell argued that Washington was already pressuring Khartoum to stem abuses and was providing humanitarian relief; applying the "genocide" label would not require anything more from the United States. He did, however, commission an in-depth study of whether events in Darfur merited the "genocide" label.

Other world leaders and opinion makers [such as leaders of the EU, Canada, and Britain] continued to show reticence about calling Darfur "genocide."

Meanwhile, other world leaders and opinion makers continued to show reticence about calling Darfur "genocide." EU [European Union], Canadian, and British officials all avoided the term, as did [then] UN Secretary-General Kofi Annan, who was pilloried in the media for limiting his description of Darfur to "massive violations of human rights." Human Rights Watch and the Pulitzer Prize-winning author Samantha Power favored the slightly less charged term "ethnic cleansing," arguing that Darfur involved the forced removal of an ethnic group, not its deliberate extermination, and that genocide is hard to prove in the midst of a crisis.

The debate took a surprising turn in early September [2004] when, testifying before the Senate Foreign Relations

Committee, Powell acknowledged that "genocide" was in fact taking place in Sudan. Powell based his determination on the U.S. government-funded study, which had surveyed 1,136 Darfurian refugees in Chad. Their testimony demonstrated that violence against civilians was widespread, ethnically oriented, and strongly indicated government involvement in the attacks. Two weeks after Powell's speech, Bush repeated the genocide charge during an address to the UN General Assembly.

Once More, Never Again

Taken together, the congressional resolution and the two speeches were momentous: never before had Congress or such senior U.S. officials publicly and conclusively labeled an ongoing crisis "genocide," invoking the convention. Nor, for that matter, had a contracting party to the Genocide Convention ever called on the Security Council to take action under Article VIII. But the critical question remained: Would the Genocide Convention really be any help in triggering international intervention to stem the violence?

So far, the answer seems to be no. In late July [2004], before Bush or Powell ever spoke the word "genocide," the UN Security Council had passed a resolution condemning Sudan and giving the government a month to rein in the militias. That deadline passed without incident, however. After Powell spoke out in September [2004], the council passed a second, tepid resolution, which merely called on Kofi Annan to set up a five-member commission to investigate the charge. The resolution also vaguely threatened economic sanctions against Sudan's oil industry and welcomed an African Union plan to send a token force to the region to monitor a cease-fire. Despite its weak wording, the resolution almost failed to pass. China, which has commercial and oil interests in Sudan, nearly vetoed the measure, only agreeing to abstain—along with Algeria, Pakistan, and Russia—after Annan strongly endorsed the resolution.

In mid-November [2004], the Security Council held an extraordinary meeting in Nairobi, Kenya, to discuss Sudan. The session won a pledge from Khartoum and the southern rebels to finalize a peace agreement by the end of the year. On Darfur, however, the Security Council managed only to pass another limp resolution voicing "serious concern." Conceivably, Annan's commission could still determine that genocide has occurred in Darfur—giving the Security Council yet another chance to take concrete action. Given recent history, however, such action is unlikely. So far, the immediate consequences of the U.S. genocide determination have been minimal, and despite the historic declarations by Bush, Powell, and the U.S. Congress, the international community has barely budged. Nor has the United States itself done much to stop the violence.

The genocide debate and the Darfur crisis are thus instructive for several reasons. First, they have made it clear that "genocide" is not a magic word that triggers intervention. The term grabs attention, and in this case allowed pundits and advocates to move Sudan to the center of the public and international agendas. The lack of any subsequent action, however, showed that the Genocide Convention does not provide nearly the impetus that many thought it would. The convention was intended to institutionalize the promise of "never again." In the past, governments avoided involvement in a crisis by scrupulously eschewing the word "genocide." Sudan—at least so far—shows that the definitional dance may not have mattered.

Second, the Darfur crisis points to other limitations of using a genocide framework to galvanize international intervention. Genocide is a contested concept: there is much disagreement about what qualifies for the term. The convention itself defines genocide as the "intent to destroy, in whole or in part, a national, ethnical, racial or religious group, as such." The document also lists several activities that constitute genocide, ranging from obvious acts such as killing to less obvious ones such as causing "mental harm." One often-cited problem with the convention's definition is how to determine a perpetrator's intent in the midst of a crisis. And how much "partial" group destruction does it take to reach the genocide threshold? In April 2004, an appeals chamber of the International Criminal Tribunal for the Former Yugoslavia addressed the definitional question, upholding a genocide conviction of the Bosnian Serb commander Radislav Krstic for his role in the 1995 massacre at Srebrenica. In that case, the tribunal concluded that "genocide" meant the destruction of a "substantial part" of a group, which the court defined as 7,000–8,000 Bosnian Muslim men from Srebrenica.

By this standard, the violence in Darfur does appear to be genocide: a substantial number of men from a particular ethnic group in a limited area have been killed. For many observers, however, genocide means something else: a campaign designed to physically eliminate a group under a government's control, as in Rwanda or Nazi Germany. The definitional debate is hard to resolve; both positions are defensible. And the indeterminacy makes genocide a difficult term around which to mobilize an international coalition for intervention.

If the international community fails to act decisively, the brave language of the Genocide Convention and the UN Charter . . . will once more ring false.

Assuming that humanitarian intervention remains a common goal in the future, one way forward would be to revisit and strengthen the ambiguous provisions in the convention. The confusion associated with the word "genocide" is not likely to disappear, however, and the term, at least as currently defined, excludes economic, political, and other social groups from protection. A better strategy might therefore be to develop a specific humanitarian threshold for intervention— including, but not limited to, genocide—and to establish institutional mechanisms to move from recognition of a grave humanitarian crisis to international action.

Darfur also shows that a genocide debate can divert attention from the most difficult questions surrounding humanitarian intervention. Any potential international action faces serious logistical and political obstacles. Darfur is vast and would require a substantial deployment of troops to safeguard civilians. The area has poor roads, and although it is open to surveillance from the air, ground transportation of troops would be difficult. International action also would need to address the complicated but enduring problems that have given rise to the violence in the first place. Such a strategy would require pressure on both the Darfur rebels and Khartoum to make peace.

Already heavily committed in Iraq and having lost considerable international credibility over the last two years, the Bush administration is not well positioned to lead such an effort. The hardest question about humanitarian intervention thus remains, Who will initiate and lead it? The problem is not just theoretical: the killing continues in Darfur and is unlikely to end soon. Until a powerful international actor or coalition of actors emerges, many more thousands of civilians are likely to die in western Sudan. If the international community fails to act decisively, the brave language of the Genocide Convention and the UN Charter—not to mention the avowed principles of the U.S. government and other states—will once more ring false.

The U.S. Congress Has Defined the Violence in Darfur as Genocide

UN Office for the Coordination of Humanitarian Affairs

The UN Office for the Coordination of Humanitarian Affairs was created by the United Nations (UN) to mobilize and coordinate international humanitarian action to alleviate human suffering in disasters and emergencies, and to advocate for the rights of people in need. This story was reported by IRIN, a United Nations news service.

NAIROBI, 23 July 2004 (IRIN) The US Congress on Thursday unanimously passed a resolution declaring the human rights abuses in western Sudan's Darfur region as "genocide".

By a vote of 422 to zero, the House of Representatives, with "the Senate concurring", passed the resolution, which stated that the violence appeared to be particularly directed at a specific group based on their ethnicity and appeared to be systemised, [French news agency] Agence France Presse reported.

The Convention on the Prevention and Punishment of the Crime of Genocide . . . obliges the UN to act to prevent genocide.

The resolution also reportedly urged the US government to call the atrocities by their "rightful" name and "to seriously consider multilateral or even unilateral intervention to prevent genocide should the United Nations [UN] Security Council fail to act".

The Convention on the Prevention and Punishment of the Crime of Genocide—to which the US is a signatory—obliges the UN to act to prevent genocide. The convention defines genocide as acts "committed with intent to destroy, in whole or in part, a national, racial or religious group". Such acts include killing; causing serious bodily or mental harm to members of a group; and deliberately inflicting conditions of life calculated to bring about the physical destruction of a group in whole or in part.

Ten years ago, the Clinton administration was heavily criticised because it failed to recognise the Rwandan genocide as such, while about 800,000 Tutsis and moderate Hutus were being slaughtered.

John Prendergast, the special adviser to the president of the International Crisis Group [a nongovernmental organization], told IRIN Thursday that new evidence suggested that Khartoum's role in genocide in Darfur was now indisputable. "The government's complicity is no longer in doubt, thus meeting the conditions as outlined in the Genocide Convention for culpability in this greatest of crimes."

The Sudanese government has admitted backing the Janjawid militias to fight a rebellion in Sudan, but has repeatedly denied any responsibility for the atrocities committed by them including ethnic cleansing and genocide.

Khartoum's ambassador . . . accused the US of trying to destabilise "a relatively stable nation", saying "it's like pitting a heavyweight champion against a child".

Khartoum's ambassador in Washington, Khidr Harun Ahmad, said on Thursday that the Sudan Campaign—an umbrella of organisations and individuals—in the US was dramatising the situation in Darfur in an election year "to take advantage of their suffering and plight to get elected or attract attention".

He accused the US of trying to destabilise "a relatively stable nation", saying "it's like pitting a heavyweight champion against a child".

"Congress has the chance to resolve the conflict in Darfur by joining hands with the government of Sudan and the international community to consolidate the measures taken by the government."

"Mounting pressure and bashing" can only lead to a failed state that is the largest in Africa, he added.

In a joint press conference in New York on Thursday with UN Secretary-General Kofi Annan, US Secretary of State Colin Powell reiterated that the US government was "examining very carefully" whether the ongoing violence against civilians in Darfur constituted genocide, but did not specify when such a determination might be made.

He added that the genocide debate was "almost beside the point". "The point is that we need to fix the security problem, the humanitarian problem. Whatever you call it, it's a catastrophe. People are dying at an increasing rate." The government had created the Janjawid so it was able to get rid of them, he continued: "Since they turned it on, they can turn it off."

The question was whether there was "enough incentive for them to turn it off. And we're making it very clear to them that there will be consequences if it is not turned off," he warned.

But other Sudan watchers say the genocide debate is of utmost importance, because of the legal imperative to act and in the light of inaction during previous genocides, such as that of Rwanda. "The debate does indeed matter, because of the implications for punishing the crime, as is called for in the convention," said Prendergast.

The Violence in Darfur Is Genocide

Colin L. Powell

Colin L. Powell served as U.S. Secretary of State from 2001 to 2005 under the administration of George W. Bush.

The violence in Darfur has complex roots in traditional conflicts between Arab nomadic herders and African farmers. The violence intensified during 2003 when two groups— the Sudan Liberation Movement and the Justice and Equality Movement—declared open rebellion against the Government of Sudan because they feared being on the outside of the power and wealth-sharing agreements in the north-south negotiations. Khartoum [capital city of Sudan and seat of government] reacted aggressively, intensifying support for Arab militias, the so-called *jinjaweid* [also spelled *janjaweed* and *janjawid*]. The Government of Sudan supported the *jinjaweid*, directly and indirectly, as they carried out a scorched-earth policy towards the rebels and the African civilian population.

Mr. Chairman, the United States exerted strong leadership to focus international attention on this unfolding tragedy. We first took the issue of Sudan to the United Nations (UN) Security Council last fall. President [George W.] Bush was the first head of state to condemn publicly the Government of Sudan and to urge the international community to intensify efforts to end the violence. In April of this year [2004], the United States brokered a ceasefire between the Government of Sudan and the rebels, and then took the lead to get the African Union [AU, a federation of African nations] to monitor that ceasefire.

As some of you are aware, I traveled to the Sudan in midsummer [2004] and made a point of visiting Darfur. It was

Colin L. Powell, "The Crisis in Darfur, Written Remarks Before the Senate Foreign Relations Committee," www.state.gov, September 9, 2004. U.S. Department of State, Washington, DC.

about the same time that Congressman [Frank] Wolf and Senator [Sam] Brownback were there, as well as [United Nations] Secretary General Kofi Annan. In fact, the Secretary General and I were able to meet and exchange notes. We made sure that our message to the Sudanese government was consistent.

Senator Brownback can back me up when I say that all of us saw the suffering that the people of Darfur are having to endure. And Senator [Jon] Corzine was just in Darfur and can vouch for the fact that atrocities are still occurring. All of us met with people who had been driven from their homes—indeed many having seen their homes and all their worldly possessions destroyed or confiscated before their eyes—by the terrible violence that is occurring in Darfur.

During my visit, humanitarian workers from my own Agency—USAID [United States Agency for International Development]—and from other Non-Governmental Organizations (NGOs), told me how they are struggling to bring food, shelter, and medicines to those so desperately in need—a population of well over one million.

[The U.S. State Department] concluded that genocide has been committed in Darfur and that the Government of Sudan and the jinjaweid *bear responsibility.*

In my midsummer meetings with the Government of Sudan, we presented them with the stark facts of what we knew about what is happening in Darfur from the destruction of villages, to the raping and the killing, to the obstacles that impeded relief efforts. Secretary General Annan and I obtained from the Government of Sudan what they said would be firm commitments to take steps, and to take steps immediately, that would remove these obstacles, help bring the violence to an end, and do it in a way that we could monitor their performance. . . .

The Matter of Genocide

Since the U.S. became aware of atrocities occurring in Sudan, we have been reviewing the [1948 UN] Genocide Convention and the obligations it places on the Government of Sudan.

In July [2004], we launched a limited investigation by sending a team to refugee camps in Chad [a country that borders Sudan]. They worked closely with the American Bar Association and the Coalition for International Justice and were able to interview 1,136 of the 2.2 million people the UN estimates have been affected by this horrible violence. Those interviews indicated:

- A consistent and widespread pattern of atrocities (killings, rapes, burning of villages) committed by *jinjaweid* and government forces against non-Arab villagers;

- Three-fourths (74%) of those interviewed reported that the Sudanese military forces were involved in the attacks;

- Villages often experienced multiple attacks over a prolonged period before they were destroyed by burning, shelling or bombing, making it impossible for villagers to return.

Sudan is a contracting party to the Genocide Convention and is obliged under the Convention to prevent and to punish acts of genocide.

When we reviewed the evidence compiled by our team, along with other information available to the State Department, we concluded that genocide has been committed in Darfur and that the Government of Sudan and the *jinjaweid* bear responsibility—and genocide may still be occurring. Mr. Chairman, we are making copies of the evidence our team compiled available to this committee today.

We believe in order to confirm the true nature, scope and totality of the crimes our evidence reveals, a full-blown and unfettered investigation needs to occur. Sudan is a contracting party to the Genocide Convention and is obliged under the Convention to prevent and to punish acts of genocide. To us, at this time, it appears that Sudan has failed to do so.

Article VIII of the Genocide Convention provides that Contracting Parties "may call upon the competent organs of the United Nations to take such action under the Charter of the United Nations as they consider appropriate for the prevention and suppression of acts of genocide or any of the other acts enumerated in Article III."

Today, the U.S. is calling on the UN to initiate a full investigation. To this end, the U.S. will propose that the next UN Security Council Resolution on Sudan request a UN investigation into all violations of international humanitarian law and human rights law that have occurred in Darfur, with a view to ensuring accountability.

Intent to Destroy a Group

Mr. Chairman, as I said the evidence leads us to the conclusion that genocide has occurred and may still be occurring in Darfur. We believe the evidence corroborates the specific intent of the perpetrators to destroy "a group in whole or in part." This intent may be inferred from their deliberate conduct. We believe other elements of the convention have been met as well.

Under the 1948 Convention on the Prevention and Punishment of the Crime of Genocide, to which both the United States and Sudan are parties, genocide occurs when the following three criteria are met:

- Specified acts are committed:
  a) killing;
  b) causing serious bodily or mental harm;

c) deliberately inflicting conditions of life calculated to bring about physical destruction of a group in whole or in part;

d) imposing measures to prevent births; or

e) forcibly transferring children to another group;

- These acts are committed against members of a national, ethnic, racial or religious group; and

- They are committed "with intent to destroy, in whole or in part, [the group] as such".

The totality of the evidence from the interviews we conducted in July and August [2004], and from the other sources available to us, shows that:

- The *jinjaweid* and Sudanese military forces have committed large-scale acts of violence, including murders, rape and physical assaults on non-Arab individuals;

- The *jinjaweid* and Sudanese military forces destroyed villages, foodstuffs, and other means of survival;

- The Sudan Government and its military forces obstructed food, water, medicine, and other humanitarian aid from reaching affected populations, thereby leading to further deaths and suffering; and

- Despite having been put on notice multiple times, Khartoum has failed to stop the violence.

Call it a civil war. Call it ethnic cleansing. Call it genocide. Call it "none of the above." The reality is the same: there are people in Darfur who desperately need our help.

Mr. Chairman, some seem to have been waiting for this determination of genocide to take action. In fact, however, no new action is dictated by this determination. We have been doing everything we can to get the Sudanese government to act responsibly. So let us not be preoccupied with this designation of genocide. These people are in desperate need and we must help them. Call it a civil war. Call it ethnic cleansing. Call it genocide. Call it "none of the above." The reality is the same: there are people in Darfur who desperately need our help.

The [Sudanese government] should end the attacks, ensure its people . . . are secure, hold to account those who are responsible for past atrocities, and [pursue] . . . negotiations.

I expect that the government in Khartoum will reject our conclusion of genocide anyway. Moreover, at this point genocide is our judgment and not the judgment of the International Community. Before the Government of Sudan is taken to the bar of international justice, let me point out that there is a simple way for Khartoum to avoid such wholesale condemnation. That way is to take action.

The government in Khartoum should end the attacks, ensure its people—all of its people—are secure, hold to account those who are responsible for past atrocities, and ensure that current negotiations are successfully concluded. That is the only way to peace and prosperity for this war-ravaged land.

Specifically, Mr. Chairman, the most practical contribution we can make to the security of Darfur in the short-term is to increase the number of African Union monitors. That will require the cooperation of the Government of Sudan.

The International Criminal Court Has Accused Sudan's President of Genocide

CBC News

CBC News is Canada's national public broadcasting company.

Sudanese President Omar al-Bashir was charged at the International Criminal Court [ICC] in The Hague [Netherlands] on [July 14, 2008] with genocide and crimes against humanity, with the indictment alleging he orchestrated the violence that has devastated his country's Darfur region and left hundreds of thousands dead.

Court prosecutor Luis Moreno-Ocampo is also seeking a worldwide arrest warrant to have al-Bashir brought before the international tribunal for his role in the five-year-old conflict.

The [ICC] charges accuse the ... Sudanese government of sponsoring militia groups called janjaweed, which have ... [waged] a campaign of murder, rape and deportation.

The Charges Against al-Bashir

The charges accuse the top leadership of the Sudanese government of sponsoring militia groups called janjaweed, which have attempted to wipe out African tribes in Darfur with a campaign of murder, rape and deportation.

Moreno-Ocampo was undeterred by concern that his indictment against al-Bashir might lead to vengeance against Darfur refugees, and the closing of Sudan's doors to relief

CBC News, "Sudanese President Charged with Genocide; Amid Predictions of Violent Backlash, UN Says It Expects Peacekeepers Will Be Kept from Harm," CBC.ca, July 14, 2008. Reproduced by permission of Canadian Broadcasting Corporation and YGS Group, on behalf of the Associated Press.

agencies and possibly peacekeeping troops. "The genocide is ongoing," he said, saying that preventing systematic rape was a key element of the campaign. "Seventy-year-old women, six-year-old girls are raped." Moreno-Ocampo filed 10 charges against al-Bashir: three counts of genocide, five of crimes against humanity and two of murder.

Sudan rejects the court's jurisdiction and refuses to arrest suspects.

Arrest Unlikely Any Time Soon

A three-judge panel of the court is expected to take months to study the evidence before deciding whether to order al-Bashir's arrest. Despite the charges, al-Bashir is unlikely to be sent to The Hague any time soon. Sudan rejects the court's jurisdiction and refuses to arrest suspects. An arrest warrant would hamper his travels to other countries, however.

"Al-Bashir now is not going to be able to leave the Sudan without facing arrest," said Payam Akhavan, a professor of international law at McGill University in Montreal and a former war crimes prosecutor. "He will effectively be in prison within the Sudan itself."

Akhavan told CBC News [Canadian Broadcasting Corporation] that in the long run, the Sudanese government might be persuaded to hand over al-Bashir—in the same way "sustained international pressure" forced the Yugoslavian government to turn in former president Slobodan Milosevic in 2001. "It may not be possible to arrest al-Bashir today, but circumstances may change tomorrow," Akhavan said. "The message has to be that you cannot commit genocide with impunity."

Al-Bashir is the first sitting head of state to be charged at the International Criminal Court. In the last decade, two other state leaders—Milosevic in 1999, and Charles Taylor in 2003 when he was Liberian president—have been indicted by other, special international tribunals set up by the United Nations [UN]. Milosevic died in 2006 while his genocide trial was wrapping up in The Hague, and Taylor is currently on trial for crimes against humanity at a special UN-sponsored court in the Dutch city.

Two other Sudanese have already had proceedings launched against them at the International Criminal Court, in both cases on allegations they contributed to the genocide in Darfur. Humanitarian Affairs Minister Ahmed Haround and militia leader Ali Kushayb are wanted on arrest warrants issued in May 2007, but Sudan refuses to hand them over.

Prosecutor Moreno-Ocampo's decision to go after al-Bashir is expected to cause further turmoil in Sudan, and some analysts fear it could make life even worse for refugees living in Darfur's sprawling camps and reliant on humanitarian aid for food and water. Moreno-Ocampo said most members of the Fur, Masalit and Zaghawa ethnic African groups were driven from their homes by Sudanese forces and the janjaweed in 2004. Since then, the janjaweed have been targeting the camps aiming to starve the refugees. "They [al-Bashir's forces] don't need gas chambers because the desert will kill them," he said, drawing a comparison to Nazi Germany's notorious method of mass murder during the Holocaust.

The refugees "have no more water, no more food, no more cattle. They have lost everything. They live because international humanitarian organizations are providing food for them," he said.

[Sudan's] National Congress Party . . . warned of "more violence and blood" in Darfur.

"Is It Easy to Stop? No"

An estimated 300,000 people have died in Darfur since conflict erupted there in 2003 when local ethnic groups took up arms against al-Bashir's Arab-dominated government in the capital, Khartoum, accusing authorities of years of neglect.

Moreno-Ocampo said the international community needs to act to prevent more deaths. "We are dealing with a genocide. Is it easy to stop? No. Do we need to stop? Yes. Do we have to stop? Yes," he said.

In an indication of the fury that could be unleashed with the charges against al-Bashir, Sudanese state television reported on Sunday that his ruling National Congress Party had warned of "more violence and blood" in Darfur. The Sudanese government has also said the indictment could affect the work of humanitarian organizations in Sudan. "The Darfur issue is an issue for the people and government of Sudan," Information Minister Ibrahim al-Zahawi said at a news conference on Sunday.

There are fears, too, that the fresh Darfur case could spark a backlash against the 9,000-strong UN-African Union peace-keeping force in Darfur. It was the UN Security Council [the main decision-making body of the United Nations] that in March 2005 asked Moreno-Ocampo to investigate crimes in Darfur.

"The country is furious and they are very angry, and they are directing this anger toward the UN, who operate a large mission here," freelance reporter Peter Martell told CBC News from Khartoum. "So the fear is that may have some implication on the mission of the UN in Sudan."

The UN said . . . it is counting on Sudan to co-operate in keeping its staff from harm. The BBC [British Broadcasting Corporation] reported, however, that the UN will withdraw non-essential staff from its mission in Sudan. . . .

Secretary General [of the UN] Ban Ki-moon "expects that the Government of Sudan will continue to . . . ensure the safety and security of all United Nations personnel and property," his spokesperson, Michele Montas, said in a statement.

Humanitarian Aid Groups Dispute America's "Genocide" Label

European-Sudanese Public Affairs Council

European-Sudanese Public Affairs Council is a privately-funded organization based in London, UK, that runs advocacy, education, and media projects that seek to encourage peace and reconciliation in Sudan.

"It suited various governments to talk it all up, but they don't seem to have thought about the consequences. I have no idea what Colin Powell's game is, but to call it genocide and then effectively say, 'Oh, shucks, but we are not going to do anything about that genocide' undermines the very word 'genocide.'"—Darfur aid worker on American claims of "genocide".

Rebutting American Claims of Genocide

Attempts by the [George W.] Bush Administration to exaggerate the extent of the crisis in Sudan's Darfur province have come under increasing fire from the humanitarian aid community and other commentators.

Certain facts are clear. In February 2003, two armed groups, the 'Sudan Liberation Army' and the 'Justice and Equality Movement', began a low intensity conflict against the Government of Sudan in the western Sudanese region of Darfur. These rebel groups launched attacks on government garrisons and civilians in the area. The government responded vigorously and the conflict spiralled out of control causing a growing humanitarian crisis. Thousands of people have died and more than a million civilians have been displaced as a re-

European-Sudanese Public Affairs Council, "Medicins Sans Frontières Challenges U.S. Darfur Genocide Claim," Sudan.net, October 4, 2004. Reproduced by permission.

sult of the conflict. Darfur is home to some 80 tribes and ethnic groups divided between nomads and sedentary communities, and the war has seen considerable inter-tribal conflict. A ceasefire agreement was signed in April 2004.

In August 2004, the United States Congress unanimously adopted a resolution labelling the situation in Darfur as genocide.

In August 2004, the United States Congress unanimously adopted a resolution labelling the situation in Darfur as genocide. On September 9 [2004], American Secretary of State Colin Powell in turn declared before the Senate Foreign Affairs Committee, "[that] genocide has taken place and may still be continuing in Darfur". These declarations echoed attempts to compare events in Darfur with Rwanda in 1994 [east African country that underwent a horrendous episode of ethnic cleansing]. Observers almost immediately claimed that the American "genocide" declaration had more to do with the US elections than the reality of events in Darfur.

One absolutely neutral source ... is the international humanitarian organisation, Médecins Sans Frontières/ Doctors Without Borders (MSF).

Any objective assessment of these American positions, given the astonishing degree of propaganda that has characterised the Sudanese conflict and particularly American-Sudanese relations, is difficult. Pressure group politics, especially within the United States, have distorted many international perceptions of Sudan. An objective assessment is, nevertheless, essential. One absolutely neutral source, perhaps the only one, by which to examine American claims of genocide in Darfur, however, is the international humanitarian organisation, Médecins Sans Frontières/Doctors Without Borders (MSF).

Médecins Sans Frontières is an exceptionally credible observer in this respect for two reasons. Firstly, MSF was amongst the first humanitarian groups to establish a presence in Darfur as the conflict unfolded. MSF is very heavily involved in the provision of medical and emergency services in all three of the states that make up Darfur, deploying two thousand staff. It has been actively assisting 250,000 people displaced by fighting throughout the region. It was therefore able very early on to form a particularly well-informed opinion with regard to claims that genocide was being carried out in Darfur. By comparison, Washington's "genocide" determination was based upon access to one thousand refugees living in refugee camps in Chad, with unanswered questions about the feasibility of impartial translation, sensationalism, political bias and rebel pressure within refugee camps. The US claim was made on the basis of fleeting, and in comparison, momentary access to approximately one percent of the total number of people to which MSF has had regular, sustained access over several months. Secondly, MSF's reputation is quite simply beyond reproach. Médecins Sans Frontières was the recipient of the Nobel Peace Prize in 1999. It has also received numerous other awards recognising its outstanding humanitarian work throughout the world.

Dr Mercedes Taty, MSF's deputy emergency director, was an early observer of the situation in Darfur. Dr Taty worked for some time with 12 expatriate doctors and 300 Sudanese nationals in field hospitals set up in the towns of Mornay, El Genina and Zalinge in the heart of the Darfur emergency. Asked if comparisons between events in Darfur and Rwanda were justified, her answer was blunt: "I don't think that we should be using the word 'genocide' to describe this conflict. Not at all. This can be a semantic discussion, but nevertheless, there is no systematic target—targeting one ethnic group or another one. It doesn't mean either that the situation in Sudan isn't extremely serious by itself." Dr Taty was also asked if the "ethnic cleansing" label was appropriate for events in Darfur. She said: "That is not necessarily accurate. There are several different tribes and clans and families and not all of them are persecuted or executed just for the sake of their tribe."

The word genocide has been used, but it creates confusion. The situation is severe enough to be described for what it is—a mass repression campaign against civilians.

In June 2004, MSF President Dr Jean-Hervé Bradol, following visits to MSF projects in Darfur, clearly challenged claims of genocide in Darfur: "The word genocide has been used, but it creates confusion. The situation is severe enough to be described for what it is—a mass repression campaign against civilians. Civilians were targeted and a large segment of them were killed. Since Médecins Sans Frontières started working in Darfur in December 2003, teams have not witnessed the intention to kill all individuals of a particular group. We have information about massacres, but never any attempt to eliminate all the members of a specific group." In July 2004, Dr Bradol stated that the use of the term genocide was inappropriate: "Our teams have not seen evidence of the deliberate intention to kill people of a specific group. We have received reports of massacres, but not of attempts to specifically eliminate all the members of a group".

There has been no outward show of intent to destroy a group of humans.

Dr Bradol subsequently described the August and September American declarations of genocide in Darfur as "obvious political opportunism". Dr Bradol has noted that there are several weak links in the genocide claim. He finds claims that "Arab" militias are seeking to destroy "African" tribes questionable, stating that "the concept of race, discarded many decades ago with regard to biology" is irrelevant and "dangerous" and has been used "outside of its historical context". Dr Bradol has also noted that "Public expressions of an intent to destroy a group of humans are no more apparent than the existence of distinct races. There are no signs of this either in speeches by the Sudanese dictatorship or in the countries' laws. To sum up: though we might suppose the intent is real, there has been no outward show of intent to destroy a group of humans, and defining the group of victims necessitates using a category that has, for good reason, been rendered illegitimate for many years."

American Political Opportunism

Dr Bradol sees a geopolitical motivation to the American move: "In the ten years from Rwanda to Sudan, what changed is the perception by the United States of the threats posed to its national security and strategic interests. And the Sudanese regime, while not at the top, figures prominently on the list of the nation's enemies drawn up by the Bush administration." Dr Bradol notes that claims of genocide have "met with great success among human rights organizations and humanitarian groups. The source of this enchantment is, in the end, just as political in nature as the unanimous vote by the US Congress."

Dr Bradol's intervention has been deeply significant. Both Bradol and Médecins Sans Frontières are simply beyond question in the authority with which they speak on the issue of genocide. He headed MSF's programs in Rwanda in 1994, and spent several weeks assisting the surgical team that struggled to remain in Kigali during the genocide. He has very firm views on genocide, the Rwandan genocide and its implications for the humanitarian aid movement: "The genocide itself tore to shreds the humanitarian movement's famous neutrality. Even when emergency aid saves lives, it cannot justify neutrality when faced with a political movement determined to exterminate an entire group of human beings. The only way to oppose such a movement is to call for armed intervention against the aggressors. That is what MSF did in June 1994 with its call, 'Doctors can't stop genocide.' Genocide is that exceptional situation in which, contrary to the rule prohibiting participation in hostilities, the humanitarian movement declares support for military intervention. Unfortunately, an international military intervention against the genocide never came to pass and the Rwandan Patriotic Front did not win its military victory until after the vast majority of victims were killed." Indeed, in 1994 Dr Bradol actively sought American and international military intervention to end the Rwandan genocide. He has pointed out that Rwanda and Darfur are "highly dissimilar".

Dr Bradol's point about US strategic interests, rather than reality, dictating what it deemed to be "genocide" has also been made elsewhere. Richard Dicker, a Human Rights Watch [an international human rights organization] expert on international law, has pointed out Washington's history of its politicisation of responses to "genocide": "In the case of the crisis in Kosovo, the use of the term was encouraged by Washington to justify military intervention; in the case of Rwanda, when there was no readiness to intervene, its use was discouraged".

In his book *Rwanda and Genocide in the 20th Century*, former secretary-general of Médecins Sans Frontières Alain Destexhe says: "Genocide is distinguishable from all other crimes by the motivation behind it. Genocide is a crime on a different scale to all other crimes against humanity and implies an intention to completely exterminate the chosen group. Genocide is therefore both the gravest and greatest of the crimes against humanity." Mr Destexhe, however, believes the word genocide has fallen victim to "a sort of verbal inflation. . .". He has pointed out that the term has progressively lost its initial meaning and is becoming "dangerously commonplace". Michael Ignatieff, director of the Carr Centre for Human Rights Policy at Harvard University, has echoed Destexhe's concerns: "Those who should use the word genocide never let it slip their mouths. Those who unfortunately do use it, banalise it into a validation of every kind of victimhood."

That the United States Administration has sought to use claims of "genocide" in Darfur for crass and electoral political reasons is clear.

Washington's ploy must be seen for what it is. That the United States Administration has sought to use claims of "genocide" in Darfur for crass and electoral political reasons is clear. In crying wolf on "genocide" the Bush Administration has not only undoubtedly banalised the concept of genocide, it has enflamed an already fraught situation in Darfur. In the wake of Washington's claim radical Islamists in Sudan have attempted a military coup, and the anti-government Islamist rebels in Darfur broke off peace talks aimed at settling the conflict. There is also no doubt that Washington will seek to push its "genocide" declaration upon the international community, inevitably causing strains once again within its European allies and the European Union.

The courage of Médecins Sans Frontières in directly challenging Washington's propaganda is clear.

The United Nations Has Found That the Violence in Darfur Is Not Genocide

Maggie Farley

Maggie Farley is a reporter for the Los Angeles Times.

A U.N. [United Nations] commission on Sudan has concluded that systematic, government-backed violence in the western region of Darfur was not genocide, but that there was evidence of crimes against humanity with an ethnic dimension.

> *There was not sufficient evidence to indicate that [Sudan's government] had a state policy intended to exterminate a particular racial or ethnic group.*

The U.N. Findings

The report documents violations of international human rights law, incidents of war crimes by militias and the rebels fighting them, and names individuals who may have acted with a "genocidal intention." But there was not sufficient evidence to indicate that [capital city and seat of government] Khartoum had a state policy intended to exterminate a particular racial or ethnic group, said diplomats familiar with the report.

It recommends referring the cases to the International Criminal Court [ICC], but leaves other options open. The United States, which opposes the court, has proposed a war crimes tribunal in Tanzania to prosecute atrocities committed in Darfur.

Maggie Farley, "U.N. Report Says Darfur Violence Is Not Genocide," *Los Angeles Times*, January 29, 2005, p. A-3. Copyright © 2005 *Los Angeles Times*. Reproduced by permission.

The report was submitted [January 27, 2005] to United Nations Secretary-General Kofi Annan by a five-member independent commission he assigned in October [2004] to investigate violations of human rights in Darfur, determine whether acts of genocide occurred and identify the perpetrators. It is not expected to be made public until Sudan has a chance to review the assessment, and until it has been presented to the Security Council, expected next week.

The commission, headed by Antonio Cassese, an Italian judge, had to reconvene after the report was completed because of disagreements over whether to identify implicated government officials who may be in charge of implementing Sudan's new peace plan with its southern rebels, said diplomats familiar with the discussions. Sudan's ambassador to [the United States], Khidir Haroun Ahmed, said he understood that the names would not be disclosed until a court had concluded that there was evidence for prosecution.

"It would not be in the benefit of peacemaking to jump to hasty conclusions and blame the government without 100% evidence because that will weaken the government as a partner for peace," he said.

The Genocide Debate

Tens of thousands of people have been killed in Darfur and nearly 2 million have been displaced since rebel groups took up arms against government forces in early 2003. Militias linked to the government are accused of numerous killings and rapes in the rebels' region.

The U.S. State Department concluded in September that genocide had occurred in Darfur based on interviews with about 1,800 refugees in neighboring [country] Chad. Their accounts indicated a pattern of targeted violence coordinated by the Sudanese government and state-backed militias, the State Department said.

But the designation appeared to put more pressure on the U.S. to act than on Sudan. The Security Council [the U.N.'s main decision-making body] has declined to place sanctions on Sudan, instead offering rewards for cementing a peace agreement in a separate conflict between the north and south that they hope would shore up a settlement in Darfur.

That peace agreement was signed this month, but the move has yet to halt the conflict in Darfur. A rise in violence has displaced thousands of civilians and obstructed access for aid workers. Cease-fire monitors from the African Union [federation of African countries with a peacekeeping force in Sudan] reported an aerial bombing by government planes in South Darfur as recently as [the previous week].

The [U.N.] committee also recommended a redistribution of land and water rights in Darfur to balance the needs of farmers and nomad grazers that have been at the root of tribal clashes.

The Role of the ICC

With the fighting continuing despite international censure, diplomats and human rights groups are seeking an effective deterrent. For many European and African countries, the answer seems to be prosecutions by the International Criminal Court.

"This is a watershed moment for the ICC," Human Rights Watch [an international human rights group] Executive Director Kenneth Roth said. "It is an opportunity for the court to show what it was made for."

But the [George W.] Bush administration is torn between its desire to bring killers in Khartoum to justice and its opposition to the ICC, Roth said. Washington is afraid that the court will be used for politicized prosecutions of Americans. As an alternative, the U.S. has proposed that the U.N. and the

African Union establish a court in Arusha, Tanzania, the head-quarters of the Rwanda tribunal, for the prosecution of Darfur's war crimes, U.S. officials said.

Russia and China, which have been the main opponents of sanctions on Sudan, have voiced tentative support for sending the case to the ICC.

Chinese Ambassador Wang Guangya said his country would help Sudan progress toward peace. Asked whether that included a referral to the ICC, he said China would defer to the African Union's decision. "They know what is best for Sudan better than we do," he said.

Sudan last week completed its own inquiry on allegations of genocide and human rights abuse, with results that on the surface, are similar to the U.N. commission's.

The Sudanese inquiry concluded that massive human rights violations by the military, rebel groups and warring tribes occurred, but that the violence did not constitute genocide. The report draws a comparison with genocides in Cambodia, Rwanda and Bosnia, and says that unlike those mass exterminations, there was no state policy with the goal of eradicating a particular group. They found evidence that government forces had bombed areas hosting armed opposition, and had killed civilians.

The [U.N.] committee also recommended a redistribution of land and water rights in Darfur to balance the needs of farmers and nomad grazers that have been at the root of tribal clashes.

The decision on whether or how to prosecute was left to a legal committee, which has not yet reached a conclusion, the report said. But Ahmed, the ambassador in Washington, said that if the international community acknowledged that rebels also had committed war crimes, not just the government and militias, then it would be "very logical" to send all the cases to the ICC. "Justice should apply to all people," Ahmed said.

Sudan Rejects ICC Charges of Genocide Against Its President

Associated Press

The Associated Press *is a global news network for radio, television, and online outlets.*

Sudan rejected genocide charges Monday [July 14, 2008] against its president for crimes in Darfur, and one top lawmaker said his government could no longer guarantee the safety of United Nations [U.N.] staff in the troubled region.

President Omar al-Bashir appeared ... at an elaborate law signing ceremony in Khartoum [Sudan's capital city], where dozens of lawmakers, diplomats and military leaders paraded past him cheering. The president waved a wooden cane and smiled as advisers danced and a brass band played nationalist songs.

Human rights groups ... fear a government backlash that could further hurt aid operations in Darfur.

Fear of More Violence

Human rights groups, meanwhile, said they fear a government backlash that could further hurt aid operations in Darfur, where up to 300,000 have already died.

Deputy parliament speaker Mohammed al-Hassan al-Ameen told state TV that Sudan was unable to guarantee "the safety of any individual."

"The U.N. asks us to keep its people safe, but how can we guarantee their safety when they want to seize our head of state?" al-Ameen said.

"Sudan Rejects Genocide Charges Against President; Lawmaker Says Sudan Can't Ensure UN Safety," *International Herald-Tribune*, July 14, 2008. Reprinted with permission.

The International Criminal Court [ICC], where genocide charges were filed ... against al-Bashir, is not related to the United Nations, though the U.N. Security Council referred the Darfur case to the court.

U.N. Secretary-General Ban Ki-moon's spokesman issued a statement stressing the court's independence and saying U.N. aid workers should be allowed to continue their work in Sudan. Sudan's government is obligated to ensure the safety of U.N. staff and property, the statement said.

Nevertheless, rights groups said they were girding for possible retaliation against any aid workers, U.N. personnel or foreigners in Sudan.

"There are risks involved and many people and commentators have warned that there could be a backlash from the Sudanese government, that they'll stop cooperating with the United Nations, that they may attack humanitarian workers," Human Rights Watch's [an international human rights group] London director Tom Porteous told *Associated Press Television News*.

Amnesty International [an international human rights group] urged Sudan to "refrain from using the (ICC) prosecutor's announcement as an excuse to block the U.N. peacekeeping mission from protecting civilians in Darfur or delivering humanitarian assistance," according to a statement from senior deputy executive director Curt Goering. "The people of Darfur have endured horrific violence for five years. The government of Sudan must put their protection above all else," Goering said.

The joint U.N.-African Union peacekeeping force in Darfur was evacuating nonessential staff and cutting back on "a limited number of operations that carry security risk to civilian staff," spokeswoman Shereen Zorba said Monday [July 14, 2008]. But all peacekeeping duties were still being carried out by soldiers, she said. The force had already increased its security posture after seven peacekeepers were killed in an ambush in Darfur last week.

Al-Bashir is accused of masterminding attempts to wipe out African tribes in Darfur with a campaign of murder, rape and deportation.

More than 20 Middle Eastern and international rights groups issued a statement calling the charges against al-Bashir "a basic step against the policy of evading punishment . . . for the horrible crimes committed in Darfur."

Al-Bashir is accused of masterminding attempts to wipe out African tribes in Darfur with a campaign of murder, rape and deportation. Judges at the court in The Hague, Netherlands are deciding whether to issue a warrant for his arrest.

The Sudan Government's Reaction to the Charges

Hours after charges were filed, Sudanese Vice President Ali Osman Taha appeared to lay out al-Bashir's defense in a news conference held in Sudan's capital, Khartoum.

The conflict in Darfur is . . . a local conflict, a tribal conflict between the various communities that are fighting each other . . . over the natural resources in this area.

Sudan is not a member of the ICC and the court has no jurisdiction over Sudan, its people or its government, he said.

"The conflict in Darfur is first of all a local conflict, a tribal conflict between the various communities that are fighting each other in order to have control over the natural resources in this area," Taha told reporters.

The vice president also said that even though hundreds of thousands have died in Darfur since 2003, the crisis resulted from droughts, land disputes and weapons flow that began long before the 1989 military coup that brought al-Bashir to power. Sudan's president "has no interest in killing his own people," Taha said.

A government committee has been formed to fight the ICC charges and resolve the Darfur crisis, he added. Sudan's parliament will also hold an emergency session on Wednesday [July 16, 2008] to discuss consequences of the ICC case, the country's official news agency said.

At least one Darfur rebel group, however, praised the charges against al-Bashir and said it was ready to help arrest and extradite any war crimes suspects. The Sudanese Liberation Movement-Unity, which has been fighting the government in Darfur, issued a statement calling the ICC action "the beginning of liberalization in Sudan."

Reaction in the streets of Khartoum was mostly muted [following the ICC action], with shops open, children playing football in streets and people commuting to work as usual. Several dozen women in brightly colored robes held a small pro-government demonstration near the British Embassy, after attempting to deliver a protest letter to U.N. offices nearby.

CHAPTER 3

Is China Contributing to the Crisis in Darfur?

Chapter Preface

China has emerged as Sudan's most important defender at the United Nations (UN) against efforts to apply pressure to the Sudan government for its role in the Darfur crisis. China's main interest in Sudan is its relatively untapped oil reserves, newly discovered in 1978. Today, Sudan is Africa's third largest oil producer, with total oil reserves estimated at five billion barrels. And because China is in the midst of rapid economic expansion, it has quickly become one of the world's largest consumers of oil, second only to the United States. This great need for oil has made China Sudan's largest oil customer and its largest foreign investor. Approximately two-thirds of Sudan's oil is sold to China. In return, China supplies arms and equipment to Sudan's government—supplies that critics say the government uses to make war in Darfur.

Although Africa holds only nine percent of the world's total proven oil reserves, in recent decades the continent has become an important source of oil because it is an alternative to suppliers in the volatile Middle East, many of whom are members of the Organization of Petroleum-Exporting Countries (OPEC), which wields significant power over world oil prices. Sudan now produces 0.4 percent of the world's total oil supply, approximately 360,000 barrels per day.

China's involvement with Sudan began in the late 1950s, but it was China's economic revolution, beginning in the mid-1990s, that created today's close relationship between China and Sudan. This revolution opened China to market forces and global trade, spurring miraculous economic growth in the country in a very short interval. Today, Africa is the source of more than a quarter of China's imported oil needs. Sudan has become China's most important African supplier largely because Western governments and companies withdrew from the country in the 1990s out of security fears and human rights concerns. This reduced the competition for China's oil companies, and China quickly took advantage of the opportunity.

Today, China is heavily invested in Sudan's oil industry. The China National Petroleum Corporation is the largest stakeholder (40 percent) in Sudan's main oil producing consortium, the Greater Nile Petroleum Operating Company, which produces most of Sudan's oil. Chinese companies have also invested in other industries in Sudan, such as hydropower and electric power plants. These investments have made Sudan China's third largest trading partner in Africa, after Angola and South Africa. China also offers substantial economic and other aid to Sudan. For example, China has agreed to forgive $80 million of Sudanese debt and to provide $13 million in an interest-free loan for infrastructure projects. China also has promised to provide $5.2 million in humanitarian assistance for Darfur.

China's official policy with regard to Sudan is one of "non-interference" with a sovereign nation. China has historically recoiled at the idea of any type of outside interference in its own domestic affairs, especially criticism of its policies of repression and accusations of human rights abuses, and it finds common ground on this point with other developing nations, such as those in Africa. Indeed, many developing countries appreciate China's protection and view the country as the emerging leader of the developing world. Critics say, however, that it is oil and related economic interests, and a desire to maintain its current relationship with the Sudanese leadership, that are really behind China's defense of Sudan.

Whatever its true motivation, Chinese support has helped to protect Sudanese president Omar al-Bashir and his government from international criticism and pressure. China has been particularly effective at blocking or watering down UN resolutions involving Sudan because, as one of five permanent members of the UN Security Council, it has veto power to block substantive resolutions. In fact, although the UN Security Council has passed numerous resolutions relating to Darfur, China has successfully blocked the imposition of economic sanctions or other strong measures on the Sudanese government. For example, although the UN passed resolutions in 2004 and 2005 imposing an arms embargo on both governmental and nongovernmental combatants in Darfur, China threatened a veto and managed to block any type of enforcement mechanism. Other UN resolutions on Sudan have met a similar fate, including attempts to impose different types of economic sanctions.

In addition, critics say China sells arms to Sudan in violation of the UN ban, helping to fuel the Darfur conflict. In fact, critics complain that the profits from oil sales to China provide a major source of funding for Sudan's government, enabling it to spend large amounts on military arms—many of which are purchased from China. Some of these arms appear to be used against the people of Darfur; both UN and nongovernmental representatives have reported seeing Chinese military vehicles, aircraft, and small arms in use by Sudan's military and the government-backed Janjaweed militia in the Darfur region.

China's position toward Darfur, however, has increasingly been criticized around the world, and this pressure has caused China to moderate its policies somewhat in recent years. In 2006, China helped to convince Sudan to accept deployment of a joint African Union/UN peacekeeping operation in Darfur (UNAMID). In 2007, China even agreed to contribute troops to the UNAMID mission. China also is carrying on increasingly forceful diplomatic efforts with Sudan on the question of Darfur, sending a special envoy to Sudan in 2008.

How far China will go to influence Sudan on Darfur, however, remains unanswered. The viewpoints in this chapter debate this question of China's role in the Darfur crisis.

China's Oil Interests Are Fueling the Conflict in Darfur

Human Rights First

Human Rights First is a nonprofit, nonpartisan international human rights organization that works to protect people at risk— refugees, victims of crimes against humanity, victims of discrimination, and human rights advocates who are targeted for defending the rights of others.

In August [2008], for the first time in history, China will host the Olympics. For Beijing [China's capital city], those will be days of pride, a chance to display its progress and bask in the world's admiration. But far from the splendor of the Summer Games, the people of a remote area in the largest nation in Africa—the people of Sudan's Darfur region—will endure more death, disease and dislocation, and this will be due in no small part to China's callousness. Craving energy to keep its economic miracle humming, Beijing has forged a strong partnership with the Sudanese government in Khartoum [Sudan's capital city and seat of government].

If China had exploited its influence [with Sudan] fully, Darfur would be closer to peace and thousands of people might still be alive.

In the last half-decade, at least 200,000 civilians have died and 2.5 million have been uprooted as Sudan has sought to stamp out a rebellion in Darfur by outfitting local proxy militias to do the job on the ground while Khartoum bombs from above. Their campaign has caused fury around the globe. If China shares such concerns, it hasn't allowed them to break its bond with the Sudanese government, a bond that provides China with oil and markets and provides Khartoum with money, weapons and a shield of legitimacy against international efforts to save the Darfuri people. . . .

It is not possible to understand why Darfur's suffering has gone on for so long without understanding how deeply entwined China has become with the Sudanese government, and how this relationship translates into support for Darfur's oppressors. China is Sudan's biggest economic partner, taking 75 percent of its exports. China is Sudan's military mentor, advising its army and giving it guns. It has leverage, a great deal of it. But it has not used that power, preferring to keep cozy with Khartoum to keep the oil flowing. If China had exploited its influence fully, Darfur would be closer to peace and thousands of people might still be alive.

The Lure of Oil

Sudan has vast amounts oil reserves, and has been exporting more and more crude to China. Indeed, nine out of every ten barrels Sudan ships go to China, reaching embarkation ports in pipelines built by Chinese companies and pumped aboard oil tankers at terminals constructed with Chinese help.

Through its state-owned companies, China controls almost all the known oil potential of Sudan. The country has 19 "oil blocks," but only nine are thought to have significant reserves—and China holds the majority rights to drill eight of them at increasing rates.

China's interest in Sudanese oil has no mysterious cause. . . . Each day, Beijing needs another 6.6 million barrels of oil to keep the nation lighted, moving and warm, the greatest thirst in the world after the United States'. Every year, China's economy expands more than ten percent. . . .

China has been Khartoum's key partner in developing the infrastructure necessary to extract and transport oil. For instance, it helped develop pipelines that stretch for more than

1,000 kilometers from oil fields to Port Sudan. Chinese state-owned companies helped build Bashair I and II, two huge marine terminals 25 kilometers south of Port Sudan that can hold 400,000 barrels of oil. Sudan owns the terminals, but Chinese companies operate them. China has also invested hundreds of millions of dollars to further develop Sudan's ability to refine the oil it is extracting.

Sudan's oil production has, by and large, been a Chinese production.

In short, Sudan's oil development has, by and large, been a Chinese production. Beijing's companies pump oil from numerous key fields, which then courses through Chinese-made pipelines to Chinese-made storage tanks to await a voyage to buyers, most of them Chinese. The development of this profitable chain has taken place in close chronological step with the mass atrocities occurring in Darfur. In 2000, before the crisis, Sudan's oil revenue was $1.2 billion. By 2006, with the crisis well underway, that total had shot up 291 percent, to $4.7 billion. How does Sudan use that windfall? Its former finance minister has said that at least 70 percent of the oil profits go to the Sudanese armed forces, linked with its militia allies to the crimes in Darfur.

In the last decade, the Export-Import Bank of China has given Sudan more than $1 billion in "concessional loans," which are low-or-no interest. Traditionally, concessional loans are intended to help poor countries build badly needed projects that are not commercially viable. Sudan, because of its oil revenues, would not seem to need the help that China Export-Import Bank provides. But by giving loans anyway, Beijing buffs its image with Khartoum, ensuring it has access to oil and markets. Beijing looks even more benevolent when it then forgives the loans as it has done on more than one occasion.

Arms for Khartoum

A long tradition of weapons transfers exists between China and Sudan. In the 1960s, China provided at least 18 Mig-17 [fighter] aircraft to Sudan. In the 1970s, it sold it 130 tanks. In the 1980s, the list included at least 20 aircraft, 50 armored personnel carriers and 50 towed-artillery pieces. Through the long civil wars between North and South in Sudan, China was always on Khartoum's side, militarily.

In the last few years, Khartoum has accelerated its weapons shopping exponentially, using its oil profits, made possible by China. While still seeking heavy weapons—such as tanks and aircraft—it has been aggressively pursuing small arms, precisely the sort a government would need if it wished to equip proxy fighters engaged in Darfur on its behalf. Between 1999 and 2005, a period that includes the start and escalation of the Darfur crisis, Sudan's overall imports of small arms multiplied 680-fold.

Observers in Darfur have reported seeing Chinese weaponry.

Observers in Darfur have reported seeing Chinese weaponry, including grenade launchers and ammunition for assault rifles and heavy machine guns. From 2003 to 2006, China sold over $55 million worth of small arms to Sudan. Since 2004, China has been the near-exclusive provider of small arms to Sudan, supplying on average 90 percent of Khartoum's small arms purchases each year.

China's continued weapons sales to the government of Sudan . . . puts China in the position of also failing to comply with the embargo.

A [United Nations] Security Council arms embargo—initially imposed in 2004 under resolution 1556 and expanded in 2005 under resolution 1591—prohibits weapons transfers to Darfur. The government of Sudan, however, has openly stated its refusal to abide by the arms embargo, claiming that it has the sovereign right to transfer weapons into Darfur, which it has continued to do. Faced with the government of Sudan's defiance of its legal obligations, China's continued weapons sales to the government of Sudan, knowing that those weapons have been found in Darfur, puts China in the position of also failing to comply with the embargo. . . .

China's Political Protection

Awakening in 2004 to just how dire the situation in Darfur was becoming, the United Nations Security Council began to think of ways to help. Its first serious response was to discuss what became resolution 1556, which originally threatened Khartoum with economic sanctions if it did not begin to disarm the Janjaweed [government-backed militia] and prosecute those guilty of atrocities. China put a stop to that effort almost immediately, threatening to veto 1556 unless all language about sanctions was stripped. So they disappeared from the resolution. Even then, China abstained from voting on the remnants of the original, as if even the revised resolution would be too much for its friends in Khartoum.

At almost every turn, international efforts to protest and end the suffering in Darfur have collided with China's willingness to stand up for [Sudan].

Later that same year, as violence continued in Darfur, the United Nations (U.N.) tried again. Once again, there was a call for punitive steps. Once again, China blocked them. Once again, it abstained from the vote on the gutted result. Once again, it said that sanctions just make a bad situation worse. A few days later, Sudanese President [Omar al-] Bashir praised

Beijing, along with the three other countries that had abstained, Algeria, Pakistan and Russia. They were Sudan's "true friends," Bashir said.

At almost every turn, international efforts to protest and end the suffering in Darfur have collided with China's willingness to stand up for Khartoum. China has consistently deflected pressure, emboldened its obstructionism and, of course, protected the two nations' myriad deals and connections. Between 2004 and October 2007, the Security Council debated 14 substantive resolutions about Darfur, and China has used its power to weaken nine of them, forcing the removal of tough language, including economic sanctions.

On March 31, 2005, the Security Council did manage to refer the Darfur crisis to the prosecutor for the International Criminal Court for consideration of possible war crimes. China did not use its veto to block the referral. Indeed, after 20 months of investigation, the prosecutor found enough evidence to issue arrest warrants for two people, charging them with crimes committed in 2003 and 2004. One was Ali Mohamed Ali Abdel Rahman, a leader of the Janjaweed. The other was Ahmad Haroun, the Sudanese minister of humanitarian affairs.

In response to the arrest warrants, Khartoum called the prosecutor a "junior employee doing cheap work." It said there have been no war crimes in Darfur, and, in effect, that even if there have been, only the Sudanese courts have the competence to deal with them. So the two men were free to move about the country. After the indictments were issued, Haroun was given a new responsibility: he became the official in charge of relief work in the refugee camps.

A Shifting Policy?

In May 2006, Khartoum and a rebel faction signed the Darfur Peace Agreement, which led to discussions at the U.N. about deploying 26,000 foreign troops to separate the rebels and

Khartoum-backed militias. Initially, Khartoum greeted the idea of a peacekeeping force with Cold War rhetoric, denouncing it as a form of neo-imperialism. China fought at the Security Council to strip the U.N. troops of the one tool they would need to keep the peace: the power to use force when necessary. China lost that fight, but Sudan thanked it for the effort. "We do appreciate the support that China has given us in the Security Council," President Bashir said on a visit to Beijing shortly after passage of the peacekeeping resolution.

Under international pressure, China began slowly to revise its position and urged [Sudan] to acquiesce to the [U.N. peacekeeping] force.

Under international pressure, China began slowly to revise its position and urged Khartoum to acquiesce to the force, though it did so privately. It pledged to assign 275 Chinese military engineers to help with the force deployment. It offered $10 million in humanitarian relief. It named a special envoy for Darfur, who even said he had told Khartoum that China was concerned that its weapons were, in fact, winding up on the Darfuri battlefield.

Eventually, Khartoum agreed to the peacekeeping force. China heralded the decision as proof of the wisdom of its close relationship with Sudan. It had used its influence for a good cause, and wanted credit.

So far, China has not paid much of a price for remaining close to Sudan, and the oil continues to flow to the Chinese economy.

But as China pushed Khartoum on the peacekeeping force last year [2007], it signed a $1.2 billion deal to build rail links between Khartoum and Port Sudan, forgave $80 million in Sudanese debt and turned over a $12.9 million loan for the presidential palace. Last year [2007], as Bashir balked at a peacekeeping force and the U.N. once again spoke of sanctions, China smothered that discussion, just as it had earlier ones about sanctions. All those steps hardly reflect a China pressuring its ally.

So far, China has not paid much of a price for remaining close to Sudan, and the oil continues to flow to the Chinese economy. But there is a real risk for China. To keep its economic miracle going, and to keep at bay democratic urges among its own people, China needs what any capitalist state needs: stability in markets and a guarantee that its investments are safe. But by consistently siding with a rogue regime in Khartoum, China puts this stability at risk. The government in Khartoum might not always be there to protect China's investments and needs, and how would the next leaders feel about China's heavy-handed role? Memories are long. The oil might not always flow.

China continues to claim that it has limited influence with [Sudan].

"China is enemy number one," said an official of the southern [Darfur] side in the North-South civil war. "They are the ones who kept Bashir in power for so long, providing him with weapons to try and win the war in the South. They are the ones who supplied him with helicopter gun ships on the attacks on Bentiu [city in southern Sudan] and other places. They are evil. They are the ones providing military support to the government on Darfur. Of course they are."

In fact, the future might already be happening. Under the terms of the 2005 agreement to end the North-South civil war, the new Government of Southern Sudan (GOSS) has the right to hold a referendum in 2011 on whether to secede. If it did secede, it would likely take with it many of Sudan's oil fields. The South has complained for years that it does not get a fair share of revenue from those fields, and has made it clear that whatever deals were negotiated between Khartoum and China about drilling rights and pipelines may no longer hold.

[China] must do more, far more, to stop the atrocities that continue in Darfur and ensure that those most responsible for these crimes are brought to justice.

If the specter of South Sudan's separation makes China nervous, it is a less immediate threat than the activism inspired by the Olympics. China continues to claim that it has limited influence with Khartoum. Besides, the Special Representative of the Chinese Government on the Darfur Issue, Liu Guijin, said China has already used its influence by urging Sudan to accept a peacekeeping force. Despite these protestations, China is clearly feeling the heat. The Chinese special envoy's recent five-day visit to Sudan is evidence of that. The Olympics are at risk of looking less like the grand ratification of Chinese success, and more like a reminder of what China has not done for Darfur.

The Chinese public relations campaign to simultaneously belittle the extent of its influence in Sudan and claim credit for playing a positive role has kicked into high gear. But if Beijing wants admiration ... , it must do more, far more, to stop the atrocities that continue in Darfur and ensure that those most responsible for these crimes are brought to justice.

China Is Violating the United Nations Ban on Arms Sales to Sudan

Olivia Ward

Olivia Ward is a foreign affairs columnist for the Toronto Star.

A dull green military truck sits on a dust-blown road. Its licence plate reads "Dongfeng Motor Co. of China."

According to a *British Broadcasting Corporation* [*BBC*] television documentary aired [on July 14, 2008], the vehicle, produced by one of China's leading auto makers, is powerful evidence that China has been breaking the United Nations [UN] arms embargo on military aid and equipment bound for Sudan's embattled Darfur region.

China is also training fighter pilots who fly its A5 Fantan fighter jets in Darfur.

Its markings, captured on film, show the truck was exported by China to Sudan in 2005, after the United Nations banned the transfer of military goods to Darfur.

And, the *BBC* program alleges, China is also training fighter pilots who fly its A5 Fantan fighter jets in Darfur, where up to 300,000 people have died at the hands of government-backed militias and tens of thousands more have been displaced.

The Issue of Chinese Arms in Darfur

The film was aired as the International Criminal Court filed 10 war-crimes charges against Sudan's President Omar al-Bashir, whom the court's prosecutor accuses of masterminding and implementing a plan to destroy three influential Darfur communities "on account of their ethnicity."

"His motives were largely political. His alibi was a 'counterinsurgency.' His intent was genocide," said prosecutor Luis Moreno-Ocampo.

In March 2005 the UN Security Council [the main decision-making body of the United Nations] endorsed an arms embargo on military aid and weapons bound for Darfur, but allowed countries to sell to Sudan.

China has consistently denied that it is breaking the embargo, and says it respects all UN arms bans.

"It's like designing a bucket with a hole in the bottom," says Brian Wood, arms control research manager for [the human rights group] Amnesty International, and a leading expert on tracing illegal arms.

China has consistently denied that it is breaking the embargo, and says it respects all UN arms bans.

"The program is strongly biased," Liu Guijin, China's special envoy for Darfur, told the *China Daily*. "China's arms sales were very small in scale and never made to nonsovereign entities."

A UN panel of five experts on Darfur, including one Canadian, has said it will examine the *BBC*'s evidence.

The documentary, produced by the *BBC*'s current affairs program *Panorama*, traces a military truck through the remote deserts of West Darfur, filming it along with a second vehicle. Both trucks had been carrying anti-aircraft guns.

"Markings showed that they were from a batch of 212 Dong Feng army (trucks) that the UN had traced as having arrived in Sudan after the arms embargo was put in place," said correspondent Hilary Andersson on the *BBC*'s website.

A witness to an attack by an anti-aircraft gun in the town of Sirba in West Darfur, told the *BBC* that it fired directly at a hut, creating "an intense wave of heat (that) instantly sent all the huts around in flames."

[Human rights groups have] claimed China was the main supplier of small arms to Sudan . . . [because of] China's growing thirst for Sudanese oil: a charge Beijing rejects.

One woman was burned to death and another "horribly injured," said witness Risique Bahar.

In another Darfur town last February, a mother of seven, Kaltam Abakar Mohammed, said she picked up some of her children and tried to run from an attack by a fighter jet—but three were torn apart by a bomb, and her 19-month orphaned grandson had shrapnel wounds to his head.

"The *BBC* report confirms our great concern that China is one of the key providers of weapons to Sudan," says Betsy Apple, director of the crimes against humanity program at [nonprofit] Human Rights First in New York.

In March the group released a report that claimed China was the main supplier of small arms to Sudan, and linked the arms deals with China's growing thirst for Sudanese oil: a charge Beijing rejects.

Amnesty International has also reported on violations of the arms embargo, accusing China and other countries of supplying weapons used to attack Darfur.

Last year it published photographs of what it says were Chinese Fantan fighter jets, along with a Russian attack helicopter in Darfur. But both countries denied any breach of the embargo.

Amnesty, and other rights groups, are calling for an extension of the embargo to include all of Darfur and the eastern part of [neighboring country] Chad.

China Has Obstructed International Efforts to Bring Peace to Darfur

Lee Feinstein

Lee Feinstein is a lawyer, a foreign policy expert with significant government experience, and a senior fellow for foreign policy and international law at the Council on Foreign Relations, a Washington, D.C., think tank on foreign policy.

The economic, political, and military relationship between China and Sudan is extensive, but not without limits. China is Sudan's number one consumer of oil and its largest foreign investor. China is an important supplier of arms and equipment to Sudan. China has also been Sudan's main defender at the United Nations [UN] and elsewhere against efforts to apply sanctions against Khartoum [Sudan's capital city and seat of government] for its role in the Darfur conflict. China has also shown that it will apply pressure on Sudan out of concern about damage to its own international standing, particularly as Beijing prepares to host the Summer Olympics in 2008.

China's fast growing energy needs have since the mid-1990s significantly elevated the importance Beijing attaches to its relations with Khartoum.

China's close relationship with the government of Sudan is part and parcel of Beijing's [China's capital city and seat of government] overall policy toward Africa, where China has recently emerged as one of the world's most influential players. China's involvement in Sudan dates to the early period of its

Lee Feinstein, "China and Sudan," *TPM Café*, April 24, 2007. Reproduced by permission of the author.

independence in the late 1950s. But China's fast growing energy needs have since the mid-1990s significantly elevated the importance Beijing attaches to its relations with Khartoum. Africa today supplies more than a quarter of Beijing's imported oil needs, and Beijing is, along with the United States and France, among Africa's most important trading partners. The political ties between China and much of Africa have also intensified in recent years, reflecting common interests as developing nations as well as common interest, in certain instances, in opposing interference by the west on human rights and related issues.

China explicitly offers diplomatic support, investment, and assistance to Sudan on a principle of "noninterference."

China explicitly offers diplomatic support, investment, and assistance to Sudan on a principle of "noninterference." That principle provides a counterweight to international pressure in support of human rights, good governance, and democracy. And, it is the principle on which Beijing bases its relations with Khartoum, despite the Sudanese government's role in the mass killings and genocide in Darfur. . . .

China Obstructs UN Action

China has been the chief impediment to strong Security Council [the main decision-making body of the United Nations] action against the government of Sudan for its role in the mass killings and genocide in Darfur, although it has calibrated its position as international criticism has grown. The Security Council has passed six resolutions on Darfur in the four years [2003–2007] since the present conflict began, but has yet to impose economic sanctions or other penalties on the government, although travel and financial sanctions have been imposed on four individuals implicated in war crimes.

The Chinese Ambassador to Sudan, Zhang Dong, explained his government's position in 2007, saying, "China never interferes in Sudan's internal affairs."

For example, China succeeded in watering down Security Council resolution 1556 (July 30, 2004). That resolution imposed an arms embargo on nongovernmental combatants in Darfur, required Khartoum to allow humanitarian assistance into Darfur, and also required the government of Sudan to disarm the [government-backed militia] janjaweed. The original draft would have established a committee to monitor Khartoum's compliance; due to the threat of a Chinese veto, however, the final resolution included no enforcement mechanism. Two months later, China succeeded in weakening an effort to credibly threaten sanctions on Sudan's petroleum sector and delayed by six months imposition of a ban on offensive military flights, which was imposed by UNSCR [UN Security Council resolution] 1591 (March 29, 2005). China abstained on a resolution (UNSCR 1593, March 31, 2005) that referred indicted war criminals to the International Criminal Court (as did the United States). The following year, China resisted efforts to sanction Sudanese government officials charged with war crimes, whittling down from seventeen to four the list of those individuals subject to Security Council travel bans and financial sanctions (UNSCR 1672, April 25, 2006). China, backed by Russia, publicly threatened to veto an initial draft of that resolution.

In August 2006, China insisted that the Security Council's resolution authorizing a peacekeeping force for Darfur include the condition that it deploy "with the consent" of the government of Sudan. In a compromise between China and the United States and Britain, the final resolution "invites" but does not require the consent of Khartoum. China and Russia abstained rather than veto the resolution.

The impact of China's successful efforts to block strong action have been significant as they are seen by Khartoum and others as an indication of continuing Security Council division on whether and if so how to pressure the Sudanese government to take action to end the conflict.

China has calibrated its position [on Darfur] as international opposition has grown.

China Softens Its Position

China has calibrated its position as international opposition has grown. Beijing played a helpful role in gaining Sudanese acceptance on November 16, 2006 of a three-phase plan for deployment of a hybrid African Union/UN peacekeeping force of 22,000 troops. Since then, as Sudan has equivocated on the meaning of a "hybrid" force, China has begun to register its displeasure with Khartoum. During his February [2007] trip to Sudan, [Chinese president] Hu [Jintao] reportedly spoke privately to Bashir about upholding his commitment to accept a peacekeeping force. In a public statement following the meeting, Hu added to China's list of guiding principles for resolving the conflict the imperative to "improve the situation in Darfur and living conditions of local people." After the visit, in February [2007], China's National Development and Reform Commission announced that Sudan no longer had preferred trade country status, removing certain financial incentives provided to Chinese companies that invest in Sudan. China's ambassador to the United Nations also publicly expressed disappointment with Khartoum following [Sudanese] President [Omar al] Bashir's March 2007 letter to [UN] Secretary-General Ban Ki-moon rejecting several aspects of the UN's hybrid force plan.

The degree to which China will push Sudan on Darfur remains an open question. There are strong reasons why China may not pressure Khartoum in a meaningful way. For Beijing, a decision to pressure Sudan would have consequences beyond the bilateral relationship, which is important in its own right. China's quest for control of and access to natural resources is presently predicated on its ability to negotiate arrangements with governments who promise it exclusivity or preferential treatment. China's comparative advantage is that it is willing to do business with governments that others spurn, and with no strings attached. A decision to pressure Sudan would erode China's reputation as a genuine alternative, which could have broader economic consequences in Africa. It would also weaken China's claim to be a standard bearer against unwanted western meddling, including international criticism of its own human rights practices.

On the other hand, China's relationship with Sudan is worrisome to officials in Beijing, especially as Beijing prepares to host the Summer Olympics in 2008. Beijing's interest in improving its international standing may shift its position towards more strongly pressuring Khartoum.

China's New Darfur Policy Is Mostly Public Relations

Jill Savitt

Jill Savitt has worked for nonprofit organization Human Rights First and directed "Dream for Darfur," a campaign to use the leverage of the 2008 Olympic Games to press China to bring security to Darfur.

The Chinese government can be very persuasive when it wants to be. China persuaded the International Olympic Committee to award Beijing [China's capital city] the 2008 Olympic Games—marking the first time in more than 20 years that the Games will be held under an authoritarian government.

Now, China is attempting to persuade world leaders, the media and the public that Beijing has suddenly become a leader for peace in regard to Darfur. But there are many signs that China's recent efforts have been little more than a public relations campaign to spare the Olympic host from continued negative publicity about its complicity in the genocide.

China's Shift in Policy

For four long years, China was a major, if not the chief obstacle to international efforts to bring security to Darfur. Beijing blocked, vetoed or diluted resolutions at the U.N. [United Nations] Security Council [the main decision-making body of the United Nations] that would have authorized a protection operation or sanctions on Khartoum [Sudan's capital city and seat of government] for continued intransigence.

Suddenly this spring [2007]—as China's role in Darfur was discussed publicly in light of the upcoming Olympics—

Jill Savitt, "China's Deadly Darfur Games: Slick P.R. Moves Around the '08 Olympics Can't Hide the Fact that China Is Still Complicit in the Darfur Genocide," Salon.com, October 4, 2007. This article first appeared in Salon.com, at http://www.salon.com. An online version remains in the Salon archives. Reproduced by permission of the author.

China took some new, high-profile steps to address Darfur. Beijing appointed a special envoy for the region. It announced that it would send 300 engineers to Darfur, and in a major turnaround China voted on July 31 for a U.N. resolution authorizing an African Union-United Nations "hybrid" force of up to 26,000 troops and police for Darfur.

Beijing insists—in media interviews and in face-to-face meetings with Darfur advocates, including myself—that its new and improved positions on Darfur have not come in response to pressure from activists pointing up the hypocrisy of simultaneously sponsoring a genocide in Africa and an Olympics at home. Beijing has said its position on Darfur is based on principle.

If China's Darfur policy is indeed based on principle rather than public relations, there is far more it could do to help bring security to Darfur.

Living Up to Its Olympic Slogans

But if China's Darfur policy is indeed based on principle rather than public relations, there is far more it could do to help bring security to Darfur. It could begin by speaking honestly about the realities on the ground there. After a visit to Darfur in May [2007], China's special envoy Liu Guijin said, "I didn't see a desperate scenario of people dying of hunger." Rather, Mr. Liu said the people of Darfur thanked him "for the Chinese government's help in building dams and providing water supply equipment."

Since then, in fact, the security situation in Darfur has gone from bad to worse. Humanitarian organizations are pulling out their personnel, and African Union forces were recently attacked and killed by a splinter group of rebels.

China could put a moratorium on oil ventures with Khartoum. Beijing contends that its purchase of oil from the regime in Khartoum—more than $1 billion each year—and its massive investment in infrastructure should be viewed as entirely separate from the violence and murder in Darfur. But it is oil revenues from China that continue to fuel the Sudanese regime's buying of planes and bombs, and its backing of hired killers, the Janjaweed [militia group].

China could suspend arms sales to the Sudanese regime, and demand that all other nations follow suit. Human rights reports document that weapons sold by China to Khartoum have been used against the innocent people of Darfur. This fact is all the more troubling given that by selling arms to the regime, China is recouping some of the money it spends in Khartoum buying oil.

China could publicly urge the regime to disarm the Janjaweed and cease aerial bombing campaigns. It could also criticize the Sudanese regime's harassment of the world's largest humanitarian operation—and cry foul when humanitarian workers are ousted, as happened recently to the director of CARE [an international aid group] in Sudan.

While China has widely touted its U.N. vote for the "hybrid" force, it has of course been silent about the central role Beijing's diplomats played in weakening the resolution—by stripping provisions that would have applied sanctions and provided a mandate to disarm threatening combatants.

China was persuasive enough to convince the international committee that it is worthy of being an Olympic host. Now it must act like one, and live up to the grand slogan it has chosen for the '08 games—"One World, One Dream"—especially when the stakes are so much greater than athletes winning medals.

China's Response to Darfur Reflects Not Only Its Oil Interests but also Its Fundamental Ideological Concerns

Yitzhak Shichor

Yitzhak Shichor is a professor of East Asian studies and political science at the University of Haifa in Israel and a senior fellow at the Harry S. Truman Research Institute for the Advancement of Peace, part of the Hebrew University of Jerusalem, Israel.

Beijing has ... been accused of protecting [Sudan] President [Omar] al-Bashir—and Chinese oil interests in Sudan—by "repeatedly us[ing] its UN [United Nations] Security Council veto power to block further sanctions on the regime." A Council on Foreign Relations [a policy think tank] January 2006 report said that China has additionally been a major supplier of weapons to Sudan, a claim elaborated upon by the June 2006 Amnesty International [a human rights group] report, titled "China: Sustaining Conflict and Human Rights Abuses—The Flow of Arms Accelerates." The report revealed that an unknown number of Chinese aircraft and helicopters were supplied to Sudan in the 1990s, and at least 222 military trucks have been sighted in 2005. To characterize Beijing's reluctance in taking more aggressive measures to intervene in the Darfur region as solely because of oil, however, would be a gross simplification of China's interests and motivations.

Yitzhak Shichor, "China's Darfur Policy," *China Brief*, vol. 7, April, 5, 2007. Reproduced by permission of The Jamestown Foundation.

Oil, Trade, and Arms?

To be certain, China has significant energy interests in the country. Sudan's oil reserve estimates of 1.6 trillion barrels are considerable, and China has invested heavily in the country's oil infrastructure. In addition to constructing numerous pipelines and refineries, the state-owned China National Petroleum Corporation is the majority owner (40 percent) of the Greater Nile Petroleum Oil Company, the largest oil company operating in Sudan. China has also invested some $2 billion into the country's Merowe hydropower dam, which is expected to provide for all of Sudan's energy needs when it opens in 2008. According to Western sources, in January [2007], Sudan ranked as China's fifth largest oil supplier with a share of 6.5 percent of China's oil imports. Yet, Sudan's reserves, ranked 33rd in the world, are hardly as impressive as Saudi Arabia's 262.7 trillion barrels, ranked 1st, or Angola's 25 trillion barrels, ranked 13th. Moreover, Sudan's oil production has been slower than expected, reaching only 365,000 barrels per day (bpd) in 2006, well below the 500,000 bpd target. It seems unlikely, therefore, that China's oil interests in Sudan are the sole consideration behind its actions or lack thereof.

While China's economic relations with Sudan are substantial, their share in China's overall foreign economic relations should not be overstated.

Likewise, while China's economic relations with Sudan are substantial, their share in China's overall foreign economic relations should not be overstated. In 2005, China's trade with Sudan increased by 55 percent year-on-year, yet its share in China's total foreign trade remained between 0.2 and 0.3 percent. In Africa, China's trade with Angola and South Africa were more substantial. In 2004, Sudan ranked 4th on China's FDI [foreign direct investment] destinations list with $146.7 million. Yet in 2005, Sudan's ranking declined to 8th with

$91.13 million. Of the Chinese accumulated FDI at the end of 2005, Sudan's share was 0.6 percent. This by no means is an attempt to minimize China's economic involvement in Sudan; the value of China's contracted projects in Sudan in 2005 ($1.33 billion) was 83 percent more than in 2004 ($725.65 million). It does mean, however, that in relative terms, Sudan is far from being a critical trading partner of China, and therefore economic concerns are at best only a partial explanation of why Beijing protects Sudan.

Sino-Sudanese military relations are far less extensive than [Sudan's] relations with other governments, notably Russia.

On the military front, China has maintained stable relations with Sudan over the years, and as Chinese Defense Minister Cao Guangchuan asserted in his public statements, China's military, the People's Liberation Army (PLA), attaches great importance to developing relations with the Sudanese army and are ready to promote cooperation between the two sides in various fields. Nevertheless, following the implementation of the UN Security Council arms embargo in December 2005, Chinese arms sales to Sudan are likely to have been halted altogether. What should also be noted is that Sino-Sudanese military relations are far less extensive than Khartoum's relations with other governments, notably Russia. In fact, Chinese analysts, attempting to deflect recent international criticism away from China, argue that the cause behind the escalation of the Darfur conflict to what is now almost a civil war, is due in large to the influx of modern weapons from other countries during previous regimes.

Beijing's Response to Potential Intervention

Beijing is undoubtedly interested in encouraging peace and stability in Sudan in order to create a more receptive environment for its burgeoning economic activities, but its approach differs from its Western counterparts. Following its long-standing policy of non-interference, Beijing prefers that internal conflicts be settled by the parties directly concerned (the government and its adversaries). As Beijing stated, "[R]esolving the Darfur issue should be realized through dialogue and peace talks." If such a domestic attempt were to fail ..., Beijing would then prefer that a regional organization take charge of the process. Only if the regional approach were to fail would Beijing reluctantly agree to an intervention by the United Nations, at which point it would have no choice but to become involved as well.

Reflecting its preferences, China's active involvement in Sudan's peace settlement began only after the Sudanese government and the former rebel Sudan People's Liberation Movement signed the Comprehensive Peace Agreement (CPA) on January 9, 2005, thereby ending 21 years of civil war in southern Sudan. On March 24, 2005, a unanimously adopted UN Security Council resolution authorized the dispatch of peacekeeping forces to the region. The Chinese were quick to comply and in May 2005, sent their first group of peacekeepers to Sudan. A more organized Chinese detachment was deployed in May 2006, and in January 2007, it was replaced by 435 PLA [People's Liberation Army, China's army] transportation, engineer and medical troops. Stationed in southern Sudan, however, these contingents are isolated from Darfur, where the conflict continues.

The stalemate in Darfur has in fact resulted in China's support for the intervention of African Union [a federation of African nations] peacekeeping forces, as well as the efforts of the Arab League [an association of Arab nations]. When visiting Sudan in early February 2007, Chinese President Hu Jintao said that "the African Union and the United Nations should play constructive roles in a peacekeeping mission in Darfur." Yet for Beijing, the situation in Darfur is fundamentally different from the one in southern Sudan. Whereas the CPA was accepted by the government as well as by the rebels—thereby paving the ground for UN peacekeeping operations—the Darfur Peace Agreement that Khartoum signed on May 5, 2006, with a main rebel faction has been rejected by other rebel groups and, consequently, has been turned down by Khartoum as well. This has been a critical factor influencing China's voting behavior at the UN Security Council.

Beijing welcomed the May 16, 2006, agreement to hand over the Darfur peacekeeping mission from the African Union to the UN Security Council by January 2007. While the Chinese delegate voted for this resolution—adopted unanimously—the delegate still expressed his country's reservations, stating: "If the United Nations is to deploy a peacekeeping operation in Darfur, the agreement and cooperation of the Sudanese Government must be obtained. That is a basic principle and precondition for the deployment of all peacekeeping operations."

> *[China's] response toward the situation in Darfur reflects not only its pragmatic interests, but also its fundamental and ideological concerns.*

Based on this agreement, on August 31, 2006, the UN Security Council approved the deployment of up to 17,300 troops (and up to 3,300 civilian policemen) to Darfur and "invited the consent of the Sudanese Government [. . .] for that deployment." Although Wang Guangya, China's representative, supported the deployment, he insisted that the "consent of the Sudanese Government" should have been obtained before the vote and should have been clearly included in the resolution. Since both amendments were rejected, China abstained during the vote. Sudan categorically opposed the UN peacekeeping force deployment in Darfur as "entirely unacceptable." . . . Fully aware of this humanitarian crisis, Beijing offered assistance valued at 40 million yuan ($5.1 million) to improve the living conditions and the overall situation in Darfur as well as a 100 million yuan interest-free loan ($12.8 million) to the Sudanese government.

Complex Considerations for Involvement

Beijing's response toward the situation in Darfur reflects not only its pragmatic interests, but also its fundamental and ideological concerns. Beijing is certainly worried that the U.S.-led efforts to stop human rights abuses in Sudan (and elsewhere) could at some point be directed at China itself. In addition, China is likely to be troubled with the implications that intervention would present for its own sovereignty, national unity and territorial integrity—ideals that are highly valued by Beijing. During his most recent trip to Sudan in February [2007] President Hu Jintao introduced four principles for handling the Darfur issue. As evidence of Beijing's concerns, the first principle that Hu underlined stated: "Respect Sudan's sovereignty and territorial integrity. Resolution of the Darfur issue will definitely benefit the process of reconciliation among ethnic groups throughout Sudan, benefit safeguarding of national unity in Sudan, and benefit regional peace and stability." Wen Xian, a senior *People's Daily* editor, elaborated that "any program or schemes for the settlement of the Darfur issue, if not favorable to the maintenance of Sudan's national unity, is bound to complicate the problem." To be sure, precedents that erode the territorial integrity of sovereign states by the United Nations are unacceptable to Beijing. For instance, in a hypothetical case of a conflict in Tibet or Xinjiang [parts of China], China would never permit UN peacekeeping forces onto its territory. Instead, Beijing would quickly and forcefully resolve the situation. Implicitly, this is precisely what they had expected from Khartoum: the restoration of stability at all costs.

It is Sudan's evident inability to do so—combined with the international pressure and the threats to China's economic interests—that have forced Beijing to convince Khartoum to accept the UN peacekeeping contingent in Darfur. From the very beginning, Beijing has cautioned that external intervention would only complicate the Darfur issue. As an editorial in the *People's Daily* warned, "The situation has worsened since some Western countries are eager to 'internationalize' what had been a pure [sic] internal affair of Sudan [. . .] The Darfur issue wouldn't have escalated so fast, we should say, without intervention from external powers driven by their own interests." Denying that any U.S. pressure has been exerted on Beijing to persuade Sudan to accept the UN peacekeeping force in Darfur, Beijing itself—though not terribly enthusiastic about the situation—ultimately favors an early settlement along these lines. Already, Chinese energy interests have been threatened, and in late November [2006], two rebel groups attacked a Chinese oil facility located between south Darfur and west Kordofan [province].

China is walking a tightrope on its policy toward Sudan.

China's special envoy to Sudan attempted to hint cautiously and delicately just before Hu Jintao's visit: "We hope that the Sudanese side could pay attention to the international community's concern." In its reports about Hu's meeting with al-Bashir, Xinhua [news agency] mentioned that the talks had been "frank," "candid" and "sincere"—Chinese euphemisms that reflect disagreements. Reportedly, Hu Jintao "has advised" al-Bashir that an efficient peacekeeping force, is required to restore peace in Darfur. Still, Beijing will by no means use threats, let alone approve of sanctions, to force Sudan to accept UN peacekeeping forces in Darfur and has stated that "exerting pressure or imposing sanctions will only further complicate the issue."

China is walking a tightrope on its policy toward Sudan. On the one hand, Beijing is undoubtedly cognizant of the repercussions that the ongoing atrocities have upon its stated interests. Not only does the conflict affect China's ability to expand its economic and energy interests in the country, but it also damages China's reputation as a "responsible stakeholder," an image that it is laboring to establish. On the other hand, however, China is also equally supportive of Sudan's sovereign right to settle its internal affairs or agree to international intervention. China is hardly likely to surrender its foreign policy pillar of non-intervention and surely does not want to become associated with the West, least of all with the United States. Consequently, Beijing has opted for the middle road, juggling its relations with all parties according to a "doctrine of the mean."

China Has Recently Initiated Stronger Diplomatic Efforts to Improve the Darfur Situation

Scott Baldauf, Peter Ford, and Laura J. Winter

Scott Baldauf, Peter Ford, and Laura J. Winter are staff writers for the Christian Science Monitor, *an international newspaper published by the First Church of Christ, Scientist in Boston, Massachusetts.*

For much of the five-year conflict in Sudan's Darfur region, Khartoum [Sudan's capital city and seat of government] has counted on the silent support of its most important trading partner, China. While Western diplomats and human rights groups pressured China to exert its influence to halt the fighting, which has killed more than 200,000, [China's capital] Beijing seemed unmoved.

China has gone on the diplomatic offensive.

This week [February 25, 2008], however, China has gone on the diplomatic offensive, opening up about past efforts and future plans. Just days after Hollywood director Steven Spielberg resigned as an artistic director of the 2008 Beijing Olympics—accusing Beijing of not doing enough to stop the Darfur crisis—China sent its special envoy on Darfur, Liu Guijin, to Khartoum ..., both to deliver a stern warning to the Sudanese government, and to remind its Western critics that they, too, could be doing more to stop the fighting.

Scott Baldauf, Peter Ford, and Laura J. Winter, "China Speaks Out on Darfur Crisis: Keen Not to Taint Olympics, and Under Pressure from West, Beijing Sends Envoy to Khartoum with Strong Words," *Christian Science Monitor*, February 25, 2008. Reproduced by permission from *Christian Science Monitor*, (www.csmonitor.com), and the author.

China's Change of Tactics

At a stopover in London, which one analyst described as a "public relations roadshow," Mr. Liu told a crowd of diplomats and China experts at Chatham House, a prominent foreign-affairs institute, that China has been "forced" to take open action on Darfur. "According to our original culture, we do a lot of things quietly," he said. "We do not like to speak everywhere. But the situation has forced me to speak out on what we have done and what we are going to do."

China's change of tactics, from quiet behind-the-scenes diplomacy to more public speechmaking, could be motivated by many factors, from a desire to maintain its paramount influence in Sudan to a need to protect its upcoming Summer Olympics. Whatever the motivations, China's diplomatic initiative carries risks and raises questions of how much influence China really has with its African allies.

"Definitely, China has found the need to play the role of global actor," says Mariam Jooma, a Sudan expert at the Institute for Security Studies in Pretoria (or Tshwane, as the South African capital city now calls itself). Mr. Spielberg's action may have sped up Beijing's diplomacy, but China looks at Sudan in much broader terms than mere public relations.

"To the west of Sudan, the Chadian rebels have been pushed back, in part with French military assistance," says Ms. Jooma. "To the south, the SPLM [Sudanese People's Liberation Movement] is hedging its bets by signing up the US as a major ally. So for strategic reasons, China is beginning to feel the need to send a message that it is quite a big player in Sudan."

As if to underscore how important the Darfur issue has become, America's envoy arrived in Khartoum on the same day that Liu arrived. Both will conduct separate talks with the Sudanese government this week.

"China has been pushing the Sudan government behind the scenes for at least two years now," says Alex De Waal, a Sudan expert at Harvard University in Cambridge, Mass. "They were a driving force behind the hybrid force of UN [United Nations] and AU [African Union, a federation of African nations] peacekeepers," which began to deploy in Sudan [in late 2007], "and it has been doing this before there even was an activist campaign over Darfur."

The combined attentions of human rights campaigners and Hollywood stars such as Mia Farrow, Don Cheadle, George Clooney, and now Spielberg may make bigger news in the United States than in Beijing, but activists have had a surprisingly stinging effect nonetheless. Beijing's response has come out sounding hurt rather than angry. But the very fact that it has responded at all is a big change.

"It is understandable if [critics] are not familiar with China's policy," Foreign Ministry spokesman Liu Jianchao said last week. He said China had played "a positive and constructive role in the proper solution of the issue" and that "China's important role in the process is widely applauded by the international community."

US, British, and UN officials have welcomed what they say are behind-the-scenes efforts by the Chinese to pressure the Sudanese authorities.

Since envoy Liu was appointed last May, apparently signaling a shift from Beijing's previous diplomatic support for Khartoum's stonewalling, US, British, and UN officials have welcomed what they say are behind-the-scenes efforts by the Chinese to pressure the Sudanese authorities.

This month, Liu reportedly told Sudan's Foreign Minister, Deng Alor, that "the world is running out of patience with what is going on in Darfur." He urged Sudan not to take actions that would "cause the international community to impose sanctions on them."

As Sudan's major trade partner, buying nearly three-quarters of its oil exports, and also selling large arms shipments to Sudan, China is thought to have special influence in Khartoum.

Mounting Pressure on China

Liu's expected mission is to parade China's achievements in Sudan and de-link the Darfur conflict from the [2008] Olympic Games.

"I think they've realized this level of criticism is really damaging to their image," said Kerry Brown, an associate fellow at Chatham House. "In the early 1990s they wouldn't have [cared]. But now they are so nervous about the Olympics, we actually might see them do something new."

Liu's trip this weekend to Sudan, his fourth since he got the job, has a dual purpose, says He Wenping, an Africa expert at the Chinese Academy of Social Sciences, a government-run think tank in Beijing. "The first goal is to keep things moving towards a solution of the Darfur issue because there have been a lot of delays," she says. "The government also intends to depoliticize the Olympics," she adds. "They do not want Darfur hanging over the Olympics."

Pressure from the West and nongovernmental organizations was not necessarily the driving force [behind China's change in policy toward Darfur].

Dr. He does not expect international pressure to change what she says is China's preference for diplomatic efforts, rather than such tactics as sanctions against Khartoum. "I don't think the pressure will lead to a dramatic U-turn," she says. "But it has had some influence. As the pressure mounts, of course the government has to respond" with "active measures" such as Liu's visit to Sudan.

International pressure has changed China's approach to the Darfur crisis before, says Chris Alden, an expert on Sino-African relations at the London School of Economics. "From a public defense of Sudan" until 2004, Beijing has "shifted in the UN Security Council [the main decision-making body of the United Nations] to successfully getting Khartoum to accept an international peacekeeping force," he says.

But pressure from the West and nongovernmental organizations was not necessarily the driving force, Dr. Alden suggests. Rather, the increasingly obvious frustration among African leaders with Sudanese President Omar al-Bashir's government (denying him the AU presidency two years in a row, and sending in an AU intervention force) was "more important," he says.

Beijing "could either be seen as going against the grain of African opinion, or getting in line with the African position, and they got in line," Alden suggests.

The new wave of pressure, however, is unlikely to significantly alter Beijing's approach, predicts Alden. "It seems they will stick to their guns against sanctions, but say they are open to any other form of pressure."

But while the Spielberg resignation may sting, some analysts say it merely points to larger problems with China's foreign policy.

"The Spielberg dilemma is a reaction to an even bigger dilemma," says Alexander Neill, head of the [British think tank] Royal United Services Institute's Asia Security Programme. "It's a grander issue. It's linked to the party and to patriotism, and nationalism, and it's showing."

Mr. Neill says, "China has to re-evaluate as a global stakeholder just how it becomes involved with countries that have civil war issues, internecine struggles, regimes that are unpalatable to its neighbors or the West."

"It is going to need some tweaking, because its policy of noninterference [with the domestic affairs of other countries] is wearing a bit thin."

Western Countries Are Equally at Fault for Enabling China's Darfur Policy

Gordon Chang

Gordon Chang is a lawyer who writes about Asia.

[In May 2007] China yielded . . . to international pressure and appointed an envoy for African Affairs. The hope in Western capitals is that Liu Guijin, a former ambassador to Zimbabwe, will persuade the Sudanese government to end the crisis in its Darfur region. Why are we looking toward China to solve a crisis thousands of miles from its borders? Beijing supports the Sudanese government, which in turn sponsors the Janjaweed militia. The Janjaweed has murdered more 200,000 civilians in Darfur and driven another 2.5 million of them from their homes during four years of conflict. The *Associated Press* calls Darfur "the world's largest humanitarian disaster."

How is China involved in helping the Arab-dominated government kill its black African citizens? It buys about two-thirds of Sudan's oil exports. About 70% of Sudan's oil revenues go to its military, which is involved in the mass murders. Yet China's involvement is not just indirect. China sells arms and aircraft to Sudan in a manner that is almost certainly in violation of the United Nations's arms embargo. As important, Beijing has used its permanent seat on the Security Council [the main decision-making body of the United Nations] to shield Khartoum [Sudan's capital and seat of government] from effective action by the international community. This has had the effect of continuing what America terms "genocide." As Darfur activists Mia Farrow and Ronan Farrow

Gordon Chang, "Darfur—The China Problem," *New York Sun*, May 16, 2007. Reproduced by permission.

recently wrote, "Beijing is uniquely positioned to put a stop to the slaughter, yet they have so far been unabashed in their refusal to do so."

If Beijing is responsible for the acts of the government in Khartoum . . . then are there other parties accountable for Darfur because they support the Chinese government?

Enabling the Chinese

So if Beijing is responsible for the acts of the government in Khartoum—and it certainly is under the common understanding of that term—then are there other parties accountable for Darfur because they support the Chinese government? As a theoretical matter, there might be. If an enabler is answerable for another's acts, then so should a party that enables the enabler.

So who is enabling the Chinese? America and other Western nations do not treat China as just another state; they actively engage Beijing and support it. For three decades it has been our fond hope that the Chinese will make the transition to representative governance and free markets from Maoism and Marxism. We have sought to help in this makeover, and, as a result, we have provided technical and material aid to China. More important, we have also been patient with the Chinese, continually tolerating international conduct that is unacceptable. We have the best of intentions, but we may be producing the worst of results.

The issue therefore arises: At what point do other nations begin to share in Beijing's culpability? The Farrows link Western support of the Olympics and Beijing's cynical policy in Sudan. With such an expansive view of responsibility it is not surprising that Ms. Farrow is now organizing a new campaign, Divest for Darfur. The goal is to cut the flow of cash to the Sudanese military. For this purpose activists seek to have [investment companies] Berkshire Hathaway and Fidelity Investments sell their holdings in PetroChina, whose parent company has oil fields in Sudan. The ties between the Janjaweed and these American businesses are hardly direct, but Darfur campaigners essentially make the argument that attenuation does not matter.

They have a point that everything is connected to each other and each link of a chain is crucial.

The Chinese may say they want the killing in Darfur to stop, yet they are not willing to take steps within their power to end it.

The Divestment Strategy

The shareholders of Berkshire Hathaway did not buy their argument—this month they overwhelming rejected a proxy resolution ordering divestment in PetroChina. The Fidelity Investment proposal is also headed for defeat. Yet the divestment idea is catching on. At the end of April [2007] the University of Massachusetts announced that it would divest companies involved in Sudan. [In May 2007] in Kansas, Governor [Kathleen] Sebelius signed a law ordering the state's largest pension fund to stop investing in companies, including PetroChina, doing business in Sudan. The legislation, modeled on a California law, also requires divestment.

China is not just about China anymore.

So should the United States "divest" China, so to speak? In theory, the principle that applies to pension fund investments should also apply to diplomatic relations. Surprisingly, we have yet to publicly talk about the moral questions that arise from our engagement of China while it helps perpetuate gruesome activities in Africa.

Unfortunately, this is not just some abstract inquiry. These days, the Chinese may say they want the killing in Darfur to stop, yet they are not willing to take steps within their power to end it. During the third week of April [2007] China's Foreign Ministry stated that it still was "not a proper time to discuss sanctions." It also indicated that it would block the efforts of America and Britain to impose them. Although new sanctions will not automatically bring peace to Darfur, they are a precondition for the restoration of order in this especially troubled area.

So it is clear that Beijing is blocking a solution. By now China has no excuse for supporting the Sudanese government. And until it withdraws its assistance to Khartoum, we should think about all the implications of our engagement of the government in Beijing. After all, China is not just about China anymore.

CHAPTER 4

What Should Be Done to Bring Peace to Darfur?

Chapter Preface

Since the start of the conflict in Darfur in the spring of 2003, the international community has made numerous efforts to end the fighting, protect Darfur civilians, address the humanitarian crisis caused by the displacement of millions, and bring justice to those who perpetrated the violence. The Sudanese government, however, has ignored most of these efforts, and with the support of China, has effectively prevented the United Nations (UN) from taking stronger economic or military action against Sudan. One of the most recent moves by the UN was to refer the Darfur matter to the International Criminal Court (ICC)—an action that has resulted in an indictment by the ICC against Sudan's president Omar al-Bashir for war crimes, crimes against humanity, and genocide.

Soon after the atrocities in Darfur became known, in April 2004, the UN spoke out about the issue, expressing great concern about the humanitarian crisis emerging there. UN officials also called on the Sudanese government to disarm the Janjaweed militia that was carrying out most of the atrocities, to protect civilians, and to allow humanitarian aid groups into the country. Since then, the UN Security Council, the main decision-making body of the UN, has tried to negotiate ceasefires, appealed and arranged for massive amounts of humanitarian aid, and passed numerous resolutions. In June 2004, for example, the UN passed Resolution 1547, calling for an immediate halt to the fighting in Darfur and establishing a UN team to visit Sudan to negotiate a ceasefire. Thereafter, the Sudanese government signed a communiqué with the UN, pledging to disarm the Janjaweed and accept human rights monitors; but it soon became apparent that these promises would not be kept.

Next came Resolution 1556, adopted in July 2004, demanding that the Sudanese government disarm the Janjaweed and bring to justice those leaders who had incited and carried out human rights abuses. However, language threatening Sudan with sanctions in the event of noncompliance were removed, reportedly because China threatened a veto. The Security Council also imposed a ban on the sale of arms to all nongovernmental entities and individuals in Darfur—that is, the rebels and the Janjaweed militias, but not Sudan's government, which many believed was directing and arming the Janjaweed.

Two months later, during which time conditions in Darfur deteriorated and the government failed to comply with UN demands, the Security Council passed Resolution 1564, authorizing the creation of an African Union peacekeeping force (AMIS) to protect civilians in Darfur. Once again, the UN did not threaten firm sanctions but instead included softer language, stating that the UN might take additional measures, "such as actions to affect Sudan's petroleum sector and the Government of Sudan or individual members of the Government of Sudan," if violence continued. When the Sudan government still failed to act, the UN's response was the passage of Resolution 1574, which included even more vague language warning that the UN would consider taking "appropriate action" in the event of noncompliance.

In March 2005, the UN Security Council finally passed a resolution—1591—that imposed mild sanctions on certain actors in the Darfur conflict. Specifically, the resolution imposed a no-fly zone over Darfur, along with a travel ban and an asset freeze on individuals responsible for atrocities in Darfur. The resolution also extended the arms ban to include the Sudanese government. In Resolution 1706, passed in 2006, the UN added to the AMIS peacekeeping force by authorizing a joint African Union/UN peacekeeping force, UNAMID.

In addition to these efforts, the UN in 2005 authorized the ICC to prosecute Sudanese war crimes suspects. This move has now resulted in a series of ICC indictments against three individuals. In April 2007, the court issued arrest warrants against a government minister, Ahmed Haroun, and a Janjaweed commander, Ali Kushayb, for their part in the atrocities committed in Darfur. In July 2008, the ICC prosecutor Luis Moreno-Ocampo indicted Sudanese president Omar al-Bashir for war crimes, crimes against humanity, and genocide, asking for a warrant for his arrest as well. This action was precedent-setting; it marked the first-ever ICC indictment of a sitting head of state.

The ICC actions may or may not ultimately result in the arrest and prosecution of those responsible for the situation in Darfur. The Sudanese government has rejected all of the ICC charges and refused to hand the men over to the court for prosecution, and most commentators agree that they are unlikely to face a trial any time in the near future. In fact, following the ICC's indictment of Ahmed Haroun, he was elevated by the Sudanese government to the post of minister of humanitarian affairs, responsible for overseeing the refugee camps in Sudan. And China is pressing for the UN to suspend the ICC's prosecution of President al-Bashir. Many people also worry that the ICC charges against al-Bashir will only produce more violence for Darfur, because the government might react negatively by stepping up its military campaign in the region. Indeed, just before the indictment was announced, the Sudanese government issued a statement predicting more violence and blood if the ICC went forward.

However, the ICC has been successful at executing arrest warrants and trying other heads of state, most notably Slobodan Milosevic (the former president of the former Yugoslavia) and Charles Taylor (former president of Liberia). Some observers also believe that the pressure created by the ICC actions may increase the pressure on the Sudanese regime to take steps to end the violence and resolve the Darfur conflict.

This legal strategy is but one of the many different solutions that have been suggested for the Darfur crisis. The authors of the viewpoints in this chapter discuss a variety of ideas for bringing peace to Darfur.

The International Community Must Act Decisively and Effectively in Darfur

Gareth Evans

Gareth Evans was a member of the Australian Parliament for 21 years and is now president of the International Crisis Group, an independent nongovernmental organization that seeks to prevent and resolve deadly conflict throughout the world.

The suffering of the people of Darfur goes on and on. This is not 'a quarrel in a far-away country between people of whom we know nothing' . . . but a man-made disaster of catastrophic dimensions of which the international community knows all too much, yet a solution for which it continues to do desperately little to provide.

The government-supported janjaweed militias, responsible for most of the atrocity crimes, have been neither disarmed nor controlled.

The Need for International Engagement

We know that since early 2003, when the Government of Sudan began its ugly counter-insurgency campaign against the newly active rebel groups in Darfur, more than 200,000 have died violently or from war-caused disease and starvation, more than two million remain displaced and homeless with another two million dependent on international assistance, and untold numbers of women have been raped, and adults and children grievously injured. The government-supported

Gareth Evans, "Darfur: What Next?" International Crisis Group, January 22, 2007. Reproduced by permission.

janjaweed militias, responsible for most of the atrocity crimes, have been neither disarmed nor controlled.

The overall situation [in Darfur] is now again getting worse: clashes between government and rebel groups are escalating.

And the overall situation is now again getting worse: clashes between government and rebel groups are escalating, one million of those in need are now out of reach of the humanitarian agencies, and the violence and misery has already crossed the border into Chad and threatens to engulf Central African Republic as well. . . . On January 17 [2007], the UN [United Nations] Country Team in Sudan warned that relief operations in Darfur, on which more than two million people are currently relying to survive, [were] in danger of total collapse due to growing insecurity in the region.

The situation cries out, as it has from the beginning, for intense international engagement—not least from the EU [European Union] and its key member states—to help reach a solution. This is a case, unquestionably, for the application of the responsibility to protect principle [R2P], embraced unanimously by the world's heads of state and government at the 2005 World Summit of the UN, and subsequently by the Security Council [the main decision-making body of the United Nations]. The essence of the 'R2P' principle is that state sovereignty is not a license to kill, and that if a state—through ill-will or incapacity—fails to protect its own people from the threat, or reality, of mass slaughter, ethnic cleansing or other atrocity crimes, then that responsibility shifts to the wider international community.

It has unquestionably been the case that the governing regime in Khartoum [Sudan's capital and seat of government] has abdicated its responsibility—not in this case through incapacity but through ill-will—to protect its own people, and has by its behaviour in this respect placed itself outside the community of decent nations. In this context it seems inconceivable that Sudan's continuing aspiration to take over the chairmanship of the African Union [AU, federation of African nations] should be taken seriously by anyone. This is an issue coming up again at the AU Summit to be held later this week: it is to be very much hoped that the continent's leaders find a way of avoiding what would be a deeply damaging blow to the organisation's international credibility.

'Reaction' doesn't have to mean all-guns-blazing coercive military intervention, although there will be circumstances . . . when anything less than that would be hopelessly inadequate.

The R2P Principle

But what does the international responsibility to protect a people at risk from its own government mean in practice? Here as elsewhere, everything depends on the circumstances. R2P is a responsibility that extends to prevention before the worst has happened; reaction when prevention has failed and the worst is happening; and rebuilding—after the worst is over, to ensure that it doesn't happen again. 'Reaction' doesn't have to mean all-guns-blazing coercive military intervention, although there will be circumstances—most obviously in Rwanda in 1994 and Srebrenica in 1995, and (most would also agree) Kosovo in 1999—when anything less than that would be hopelessly inadequate. There are situations where a full-scale ground invasion, even if the will and resources for it could be found, would actually do more harm than good—and this may be the case in Sudan, given the probability that it would lead both to the immediate collapse of life-saving relief operations in Darfur, and of the whole laboriously constructed but very fragile north-south peace process.

But that still leaves a great deal of scope here for the R2P principle to apply in reaction to what has been happening. To stop the present carnage, and its extension into neighbouring countries, there are political and diplomatic and legal and coercive economic levers to be engaged, and a whole range of military measures: peacekeeping forces that are armed with strong and effective civilian protection mandates and actually carrying them out, and—more coercively, but still falling short of outright ground invasion—the enforcement of no fly zones. And to secure any kind of sustainable peace, there has to be not only a more credible and comprehensive peace agreement negotiated by all the relevant players—with strong international engagement and support—but a far-reaching and effective post-conflict reconciliation process set in train. . . .

What is needed . . . [in Darfur is]:

- a secure environment and a return to law and order that allows the displaced to return to their homes;

- a sustainable political agreement that is embraced by all armed groups and that deals with the root causes of the conflict; and

- a process for reconciliation and accountability that allows the people of Darfur to live at peace once again. . . .

Past Efforts Have Failed

We have to frankly acknowledge that, for all the efforts over the last three years or more . . . the international community has failed to act decisively and effectively since the Darfur crisis began. There has been much talk—both at the level of high-blown rhetoric (of which we have had too much), and hard, slogging, hands-on negotiation (of which we have had rather too little)—but almost no effective action to show for it, both at the political settlement and physical civilian protection levels.

The situation cries out, as it has from the beginning, for intense international engagement to help achieve a fully observed ceasefire, a sustainable political settlement, and, above all, to provide effective civilian protection, immediately and through the long transition back to normality.

From time to time all these objectives have seemed within reach. A Ceasefire Agreement brokered by the African Union was signed in April 2004, and the Security Council demanded in July 2004 that the Government of Sudan disarm the janjaweed militias and bring to justice their leaders. But ever since the ceasefire has been systematically violated, and the Security Council directive ignored.

In May [2006], under immense pressure from the U.S. and others, a Darfur Peace Agreement (DPA) was negotiated and signed by the government and one key rebel group. But it has since become clear that the gambit of pressuring Minni Minawi [a rebel leader] to sign has comprehensively failed. The agreement left unresolved critical local grievances (especially as to compensation and power sharing), won no effective local support, and has been followed by an intensification rather than a cessation of the fighting. And local and international efforts to bring the splintering rebel groups together into some kind of united negotiating front have so far borne zero fruit.

The failed DPA has left a political vacuum that still has yet to be filled. And so long as it remains unfilled there seems little point in pursuing the Darfur-Darfur Dialogue and Consultation (DDD-C) provided for under the DPA. . . . The political agreement and reconciliation processes are a natural continuum, with the latter premised on genuine support for the former: looked at this way, pushing forward with the DDD-C in the current environment, as the NCP [National Congress Party, Sudan's ruling government] wants to do, will not only not succeed but tend to poison the credibility of the whole process.

Effective civilian protection is another crucial objective which looked achievable for a time. After the African Union's 7000-strong African Mission in Sudan (AMIS) force was first deployed in August 2004, at least in and around the displaced persons camps a significant measure of security was provided, and a huge humanitarian relief operation was able to be mounted. But the shortcomings of the AMIS mission—in terms of troop numbers, mandate, command and control, logistic support and general capacity to sustain the protective effort month in and month out—had became increasingly obvious by late 2005.

As a result, efforts have been directed for the last thirteen months [to] getting the AU force replaced, or at least supplemented, by a new UN force which would bring the numbers on the ground up to at least 20,000: not very many for a region the size of France, but with the right professionalism, equipment and mobility maybe just enough.

Those efforts have, however, been constantly frustrated by [Sudanese] President [Omar al] Bashir and his government allies. He has refused point blank to comply with UN Security Council resolution 1706 of August 2006 which 'invites the consent' of the Government of Sudan to the deployment to Darfur of 20,600 military and civilian personnel as an extension of the existing UN Mission in Sudan (UNMIS), established to monitor the Comprehensive Peace Agreement (CPA) which brought to an end the disastrous 20 year North-South conflict.

Under pressure to compromise from the African Union and Arab League among others, the UN agreed in Addis Ababa on 16 November [2006] to abandon the UNMIS extension proposal in favour of a 'hybrid' AU-UN force—built up over three phases, 'of a predominantly African character', with 'backstopping and command and control structures provided by the UN', and an ultimate force strength of 17,000 peacekeepers and 3,000 police. But President Bashir and his government continue duck and weave on what new international protective force, if any, they will accept. He sent a letter to [then-secretary general of the UN] Kofi Annan on 23 December 2006 accepting the 'hybrid' force, along with whatever force parameters were decided upon by the UN and AU. Yet since that time the President and senior government officials have continued to publicly refuse any significant UN involvement in Darfur, once again directly contradicting Bashir's earlier commitment.

It has been clear for a long time that President Bashir is simply toying with the international community. All attempts to persuade and engage him have manifestly failed. [New Mexico] Governor Bill Richardson claimed some success in Sudan [in January 2007] . . . in getting President Bashir to agree to a 60-days ceasefire to enable preparations for a political settlement to advance, and also to some other concessions on humanitarian aid and media access. But this new ceasefire commitment seems to be already going the way of those of the past, with no noticeable change on the ground and attacks continuing, including a reported lethal government bombing raid in North Darfur . . . on 20 January [2007]. It seems unlikely that ad hoc diplomatic or individual initiatives of this kind will ever bear much fruit.

What we do know is that the international community has not been good at matching persuasion with hard pressure. Persuasion without such pressure is only rarely successful, and it's time for the screws to be really tightened on Khartoum.

Over and again, when it has come to reining in the janjaweed or ceasing aerial assaults or cooperating with international protective efforts, the Security Council has until now said 'do this or else'—and then not delivered on the 'or else'. The US government spoke of a 1 January 2007 deadline for [Sudan's] acceptance of the hybrid force, which Bashir's 23 December [2006] letter arguably accommodates. But the continued public denials, and continued government attacks and aerial bombing raids in Darfur throughout the month of January [2007] paint a very different picture. It is now crystal clear that the threshold for more robust measures against the government has been passed.

A Range of Measures Needed

In addition to the International Criminal Court continuing to pursue and extend its investigations, and threatening robust action against any future atrocity crimes, there are a range of strong economic measures which, if implemented or even credibly threatened, could fundamentally change the cost-benefit calculation of the National Congress Party leadership in favor of cooperation. For the most part they have been flagged already, at least in general terms, by earlier Security Council resolutions. They include:

- extension of targeted sanctions (involving primarily travel bans and asset freezes) on all the individuals named in the UN's own Commission of Inquiry and Panel of Experts reports;

- measures specifically targeting revenue flows from the petroleum sector, and foreign investment in and supply of goods and services to that and associated sectors; and

- authorization by the Security Council of an investigation of the offshore accounts of government majority party-affiliated businesses, to pave the way for sanctions against the regime's commercial entities, the main conduit for financing militias.

Thus far the Security Council has been largely unwilling to implement these steps. Not surprisingly, the governing NCP regime's behavior in Darfur remains the same, based on its belief that it can continue to get away with murder without consequences from the international community. EU countries in the Security Council (the UK and France, with Belgium and Italy as the current non-permanent members) must take the lead, together with the U.S. to push for the implementation of these kinds of measures, particularly the targeted sanctions that have already been recommended by the UN appointed bodies.

In the case of Darfur, . . . [the international community must] be absolutely sure that the application of military force will not do more harm than good.

The EU can certainly do much on its own, or in partnership with other willing countries, to hold the Government of Sudan accountable through targeted punitive measures. If tough new measures are to be applied against Khartoum, it is critically important that they be as broad-based as possible. Here, the EU can lead effectively in reversing the international apathy. The EU must move beyond its pattern of public condemnation for active government recruitment and support of armed militias, continuing bombing campaign, and double-talk on the deployment of a hybrid force, to more meaningful steps.

EU Foreign Ministers should set out a clear and detailed set of public benchmarks for the Sudanese government to comply with, including:

- full Sudanese cooperation with all aspects of the deployment of the hybrid force;

- immediate cessation of its military offensive in Darfur;

- immediate cessation of aerial bombardment;

- the lifting of bureaucratic obstacles to humanitarian relief and the AU; and

- steps showing re-engagement in good faith in a revamped peace process.

Failure to achieve these benchmarks should trigger EU wide travel bans against NCP leaders; bans on European companies operating in or facilitating operations in Sudan's oil sector; and a freeze on any NCP controlled assets or NCP owned companies operating within the EU.

Military measures remain far more problematic. As I have already indicated, there is a real difficulty with any more robust application of non-consensual military force—a full ground-based 'humanitarian intervention' of the kind that some have been calling for—although that is not to say that contingency planning should not take place (and be seen to be taking place) for such an eventuality. There are five prudential criteria, or criteria of legitimacy, that should always be satisfied before any military force is applied against a country's will: the seriousness of the harm being responded to, right intention, last resort, proportionality of response, and balance of consequences. In the case of Darfur, the last of these—the need to be absolutely sure that the application of military force will not do more harm than good, is the hardest to satisfy. On all available evidence, a ground invasion would not only be a nightmare to effectively implement, but would lead to the collapse of the extremely fragile north-south CPA, and make impossible the work of the humanitarian agencies in Darfur, in both cases with devastating human consequences.

All that said, there is one coercive military measure for which the EU and others should be pushing hard, one falling well short of full-scale ground invasion, and as such not quite so problematic, though clearly much more intrusive than the extended peacekeeping force—AU, UN or hybrid—that has been the focus of the debate so far. And that is for the Security Council to back its 2005 demand that the Sudanese government cease 'offensive military flights' over Darfur with the immediate establishment of a No Fly Zone if aerial attacks on civilians again intensify.

As I and a number of former foreign ministerial colleagues from around the world—including [former U.S. secretary of state] Madeleine Albright and [German former foreign minister] Joschka Fischer—said in a statement published in the *Financial Times* on 18 December [2006], the 'Darfur conflict is more complex than often characterized. It does not simply reflect, but rather cuts across tribal, Arab v. African ethnic, and farmer v. herder stereotypes. It is coloured by local grievances and aggravated by greed, which takes the form of banditry and competition for scarce resources.'

But we were very clear about the bottom line: 'The primary cause of the ongoing crisis, however, remains the callousness of the governing elite, intent on preserving its own privileges and indifferent to its population.'

The suffering and misery of the people of Darfur have gone on too long.

The suffering and misery of the people of Darfur have gone on too long. The excuses of Khartoum and those who would support it have long since exhausted credibility. It is time for Sudan to rejoin the community of nations respected for their commitment to the highest standard and values, and for the international community, once and for all and without further excuses of its own—and with the EU and its key member states playing a leading role—to act decisively and effectively to persuade it to do so.

The International Community Must Ensure the Success of the UN Peacekeeping Force in Darfur

Jerry Fowler and John Prendergast

Jerry Fowler is president of the Save Darfur Coalition, an alliance of over 100 advocacy and humanitarian organizations seeking peace in Darfur. John Prendergast is co-chair of Enough, a project of the Center for American Progress that seeks to end genocide and crimes against humanity.

The United Nations-African Union mission in Darfur, known as UNAMID, is stunted. Only one-third of the troops are deployed, critical gaps exist in equipment and logistical support and the force has been repeatedly attacked. The Sudanese government systematically obstructs full deployment with total impunity.

A number of interrelated challenges . . . threaten to set the entire nation of Sudan on fire.

The inability to deploy UNAMID is but one of a number of interrelated challenges that threaten to set the entire nation of Sudan on fire. These include the recent attack by Darfurian rebels on Khartoum [Sudan's capital city] and the worsening violence in Darfur; the destruction of the politically important and oil-rich town of Abyei by Sudanese government troops and allied militias; the faltering Comprehensive Peace Agreement which ended the decades long war between the north and south; and an ongoing proxy war between Chad and Sudan. . . .

Jerry Fowler and John Prendergast, "Keeping Our Word: Fulfilling the Mandate to Protect Civilians in Darfur," ENOUGH, www.enoughproject.org, June 16, 2008. Reproduced by permission.

If fully deployed and fully capable, UNAMID can save lives and protect civilians. For UNAMID to effectively provide protection and stability for the people of Darfur, however, it must be coupled with an inclusive peace process that is mindful of the interconnected crises in Sudan.

The world promised Darfur protection, but has failed to deliver it.

The world promised Darfur protection, but has failed to deliver it. The Security Council [the main decision-making body of the United Nations] risks signaling that it is more serious about protecting the interests of repressive governments than in promoting global peace and security. To reverse this, the Security Council must lead in ensuring that UNAMID has all of the equipment and personnel it needs, and create real costs for those officials—government, rebel or militia—that would undermine peace, protection and justice in Sudan.

To date, the international community has not demonstrated the political will for UNAMID to succeed. It has not mounted an effective peace process to create the space for the force to achieve its ultimate goal of a stable Darfur. There are concrete steps world leaders must take in the short term to overcome UNAMID's logistical and political obstacles and secure the lives and livelihoods of Darfur's people.

UNAMID in the Field

The United Nations-African Union hybrid command assumed official control of international peacekeeping operations in Darfur on December 31, 2007. It replaced a poorly equipped and ineffective A.U. [African Union, a federation of African nations] force command structure but retained the A.U. troops. By June 5, 2008, the United Nations [U.N.] had added only a few hundred additional troops of the seventeen-thousand troops authorized to deploy. The Sudanese government and critical shortfalls in equipment hamper the force at every turn.

Despite these challenges, UNAMID has improved the breadth and quality of civilian protection. According to the most recent report to the Security Council from U.N. Secretary-General Ban Ki-moon, "[b]oth the military and . . . police components have expanded confidence-building patrols, which now cover more than 80 per cent of . . . camps in Darfur. In addition, patrols times have been extended."

By maintaining a visible presence, these patrols play an essential role in making people feel more secure. During patrols, UNAMID troops and police engage with community leaders on security concerns and pay visits to essential service points. These improvements raise the hope that when fully deployed, UNAMID may significantly increase protection for Darfuri civilians.

UNAMID's gains, however, are dangerously modest. Luis Moreno Ocampo, chief prosecutor of the International Criminal Court, recently reported to the Security Council that "civilians are being killed, houses burned and looted, markets and schools bombed, mosques destroyed," underscoring the perilous situation in Darfur. Moreno Ocampo further stated that the "crimes are conducted in a systematic and identical manner throughout Darfur." Violence and insecurity displaced between 130,000 and 140,000 Darfuris since the beginning of 2008, some for the second and third time.

UNAMID still has no presence in some camps, and minimal presence in some of the remote villages that need it most. Although UNAMID has expanded confidence-building patrols, the force is not conducting extended, multi-day patrols. Daily patrols start after breakfast and end before dinner because the troops do not have the ability to sustain themselves with food and water for long periods of time. Around Nyala in South Darfur, UNAMID has enough resources only to patrol the ten internally displaced persons camps closest to the city center.

Bandits, rebel groups and the Sudanese army have attacked UNAMID at least four times. On January 8, 2008 the Sudanese Armed Forces shot at a UNAMID convoy, killing a driver. Force personnel have never returned fire during an attack. In one instance they were unarmed. In the most recent attack, a UNAMID police officer was killed in his vehicle while on duty. Each unanswered attack on UNAMID reinforces the perception that it cannot even protect itself, let alone the civilians in its care, harming its credibility with the civilian population it was sent to protect.

UNAMID in its present form cannot fulfill its mandate.

Sudanese Government Obstructions

The Sudanese government is the biggest threat to UNAMID. Khartoum has obstructed every attempt to deploy peacekeepers to Darfur, starting with the original A.U. mission. The government refused to accept the U.N. mission authorized under Security Council Resolution 1706 in 2006. They consented to the weaker UNAMID hybrid force in 2007, authorized by the new resolution 1769. But while the government accepted UNAMID in word, it persistently obstructs its deployment in deed.

Khartoum has erected a labyrinth of bureaucratic hurdles that block UNAMID's progress even while it feigns cooperation.

Khartoum [Sudan's capital city and seat of government] has erected a labyrinth of bureaucratic hurdles that block UNAMID's progress even while it feigns cooperation. Together, these obstructions delayed the force for over ten months. Among these obstructions are:

1. *Troops.* The Sudanese government has not approved the list of troop contributing countries submitted by the African Union and the United Nations last October [2007]. Khartoum made ambiguous statements about allowing additional African battalions, a Thai battalion and two Nepalese companies, but no firm commitments. Responding to Sudanese government pressure, UNAMID expelled a British general who was a senior UNAMID official in late May [2208]. The general's expulsion was reportedly because of his nationality and assertive work to implement UNAMID's mandate.

2. *Land.* There is not sufficient land allocated to construct bases, barracks and other vital facilities. The force needs land in numerous locations with sufficient access to water for new bases and to expand existing bases. The government must provide land before UNAMID can begin the long process to plan and construct the facilities.

3. *Flights.* Despite signing a Status of Forces Agreement (SOFA) to allow for unrestricted UNAMID flight privileges, the United Nations reported in April [2008] that the government refuses its flights at night, effectively limiting UNAMID's ability to move freely to fulfill its mandate. After the rebel Justice and Equality Movement attacked Khartoum on May 10, 2008, the government closed airports in Darfur for at least three days, cancelling all UNAMID flights.

> On two separate occasions in April and May [2008], the force was left with no choice but to evacuate injured civilians by road after government forces conducted aerial bombardments on several villages. The process was not only slow and inefficient, but unnecessarily dangerous. The recent bombardment of the village of Shigeg Karo, which killed up to 13 people, including 6 children, illustrates the detrimental effects

of flight restrictions to the effectiveness of the force. Due to government restrictions and its unwillingness or inability to provide safe passage for UNAMID, responders did not reach the village for three days. As a result injured civilians with treatable wounds died, and others reportedly drove themselves to distant hospitals.

UNAMID's rapid response capability is as crucial as the proactive patrols it undertakes, especially because it is currently understaffed and simply cannot be in all places at all times. It is vital that UNAMID be able to rapidly move assets, evacuate personnel and civilians and to monitor government and militia movement and violations through aerial surveillance.

4. *Equipment.* Before making a seven week journey to Darfur, equipment arrives at Port Sudan in eastern Sudan. It takes four weeks on average for the government to release equipment from Port Sudan and critical equipment has been repeatedly held up in customs. Troops can not deploy until specific pieces of equipment are in place and certain facilities are up and running. The government has refused to provide sufficient security for equipment travelling through territories it controls, slowing its movement and leaving convoys open to banditry and attacks.

Some previously resolved problems also continue to delay the force. The Sudanese government did not sign the SOFA governing the operation of UNAMID for six months after the U.N. authorized the force. The six-month refusal created hesitation for countries to provide troops, police and equipment, creating critical gaps that continue to plague the mission today. Worse yet, government approval of the SOFA has yet to translate into actual enforcement. SOFA authorizes UNAMID to move freely by land or air, but in practice government obstructions have prevented it from effectively exercising this authority. So far, the United Nations has not presented measures that hold the government accountable for violations of the letter and spirit of the SOFA.

The U.N. Security Council must demand Khartoum's unconditional cooperation with UNAMID and create real consequences for any further obstruction. Individuals in the Sudanese government responsible for any future obstruction should be sanctioned immediately. Sanctions should be removed only when clear benchmarks are met and the force is clearly viable and has deployed.

The Security Council has a clear choice. It can demand Khartoum's cooperation and impose real costs for intransigence. Or, it can continue to stand idly by and tolerate Khartoum's obstruction.

Missing Resources

Government obstruction is UNAMID's primary obstacle, but the force also lacks critical resources and capabilities. Even fully deployed, UNAMID can not improve security in Darfur unless troops can travel from their bases, communicate throughout the region, quickly gather intelligence, and rapidly respond to security incidents. To meet these needs, UNAMID urgently requires assets including:

1. Eighteen medium transport helicopters and at least four more tactical helicopters. Without them, UNAMID will have limited rapid-response capability and will be unable to reach many areas.

2. Aerial reconnaissance so the force can monitor and verify events and respond accordingly.

3. Medium and heavy transport tracks to move personnel and materials throughout the rugged terrain.

4. Additional engineers to build and expand installations necessary for troop deployment.

5. Multi-role logistical support units critical to the deployment and sustainability of infantry battalions.

Once these assets are identified and committed, it will still take months for the equipment to reach Darfur. Contributions must be made now for UNAMID to fulfill its mandate by the end of 2008.

If the force does not receive the necessary equipment and logistical resources, there is a real danger that the force will fail. U.N. member states must supply the mission they authorized right away. If they do not, UNAMID's failure will be their responsibility.

It is also imperative that training for UNAMID's African infantry battalions continue in tandem with the procurement effort. The U.S., France, and the UK are training and equipping African forces from Ethiopia, Rwanda, Malawi, Senegal, Ghana, Tanzania, Nigeria, and Burkina Faso in preparation for their duty in Darfur. The train-and-equip effort should prepare police units and additional troops as well.

Gender sensitivity and sexual violence prevention and response training should also be included. Systematic sexual violence is a major part of Darfur's insecurity. While the United Nations Development Programme is currently training soldiers and police in programs on gender-sensitivity and sexual violence, these programs need to be expanded. Police units must receive special training in these areas because they will interact with civilians most closely on a daily basis.

Bureaucratic Hurdles at the U.N.

The U.N.'s Department of Peacekeeping Operations (DPKO) is working daily to organize and deploy UNAMID. It is the largest U.N. peacekeeping mission in history and it will work in one of the least hospitable places on the planet. It's a Herculean task. U.N. member states must provide the force's resources, but DPKO also needs to act with more determination.

When the U.N. took over Darfur peacekeeping operations, it cancelled most of the African Union's multi-role logistics contract with a private U.S. company for services such as meals, water and vehicle maintenance. In June [2008], the Sudanese government announced that they were seeking to terminate the full contract. More recently, the Government of Sudan banned U.S. companies from doing business with the peacekeeping force in Sudan. The United Nations has been planning for a peacekeeping mission in Darfur since 2006, but reports indicate that a new contract may not be in place before the end of 2008. This is simply unacceptable.

The United Nations must accelerate a contract for sustainment services and logistical support, and must not accept government interference with its implementation. The majority of battalions from African countries do not have the capacity to sustain themselves in the field. Some new, otherwise ready UNAMID battalions are unable to deploy because of this incapability. Most currently deployed battalions can not venture far from their bases. The United Nations has both the ability and the funding available to award such a contract sooner than the end of 2008.

DPKO must also work more quickly to build camps and barracks for additional troops, and must demonstrate flexibility in considering technical specifications for helicopters. The Concept of Operations breaks Darfur into three very large sectors of operation, with central basing for helicopters. The distances from the central hub to the edges of the sectors are too great for many helicopters to cover. As a result, it prevents possible contributors from providing helicopters and leaves only Russian-designed helicopters as suitable. If non-Russian design helicopters become available for the mission, DPKO should be willing to revise their plans to accommodate other helicopters.

Breaking the Deadlock

The primary impediment to full deployment of a capable UNAMID force is the Sudanese government. But the international community's failure to provide necessary resources and bureaucratic hurdles at the United Nations are also to blame. Ultimately, the fate of UNAMID now falls on the shoulders of the U.N. Security Council member states that authorized it, especially its permanent five members. They must now demand compliance from Khartoum, contribute the necessary resources, and ensure swift implementation by the United Nations.

Tolerance in the face of clear obstruction of a U.N. Security Council resolution is unacceptable. It leaves the people of Darfur in peril and risks the credibility of the United Nations and of peacekeeping operations as a whole. Patience in the face of U.N. bureaucratic obstacles slows deployment and undermines the mission's effectiveness.

The U.N. Security Council can and must summon the political will to act on behalf of Darfur and on behalf of the global peace it is mandated to protect. There are several urgent steps that can be taken:

1. The United States should use its Security Council presidency in June to convene a special session of the council, the Friends of UNAMID working group of nations, and the U.N. Department of Peacekeeping Operations to overcome logistical and resource issues. The conference should be open to the public to hold member states accountable.

2. The Security Council should pass a second resolution on UNAMID setting clear benchmarks and targets for deployment.

3. The Security Council should impose sanctions on individuals, in or out of the Sudanese government, who obstruct deployment.

4. The Security Council should exercise stronger oversight of the DPKO to ensure that bureaucratic hurdles are swiftly resolved.

5. UNAMID should assign a military attorney to actively monitor implementation of the SOFA, as well other obstructions or violations by the government, its proxy militias, rebels and common criminals.

Humanitarian conditions are deteriorating, violence is escalating, and security throughout Sudan is uncertain.

The U.N.'s Credibility at Stake

In May [2008], Secretary General Ban Ki-moon offered a plan to deploy 80 percent of UNAMID by the end of 2008. Even this underwhelming goal will require urgent and steadfast action to accomplish.

Humanitarian conditions are deteriorating, violence is escalating, and security throughout Sudan is uncertain. The fate of millions of people in Darfur is at stake. By unanimously authorizing UNAMID, the U.N. Security Council tied itself and its credibility to the future of that mission. Almost a year of rhetoric from world leaders since that date has not resulted in substantial improvements on the ground in Darfur, leaving UNAMID's success in doubt.

The greatest tests of U.N.-A.U. cooperation for years to come will be the effective deployment of the hybrid force in Darfur and the conclusion of a sustainable peace agreement. A failure to fully deploy UNAMID right away will undermine any future U.N.-A.U. initiatives and threatens the credibility of both institutions. Civilians in other African conflict zones will feel the effects of this joint model's success or failure for years to come.

The International Community Must React to the New Reality in Darfur

David Mozersky

David Mozersky is the Horn of Africa project director at the International Crisis Group, an independent nongovernmental organization that seeks to prevent and resolve deadly conflict throughout the world.

Darfur has dropped out of Western headlines again for the moment, eclipsed by events in Pakistan, the Middle East and Iraq. But while the erratic attention of the international community is focused elsewhere, the seeds of Sudan's next civil war are being planted. And the costs of global complacency are growing intolerably high.

The Darfur situation has evolved . . . into a conflict increasingly marred by shifting alliances, regional meddling and a growing complex tribal dimension.

Deteriorating Conditions in Darfur

In just a few years, the Darfur situation has evolved from a rebellion with defined political aims and a clear set of actors, into a conflict increasingly marred by shifting alliances, regional meddling and a growing complex tribal dimension. The main constant has been the actions of Khartoum's ruling National Congress Party, which continues to pursue destructive policies in the region. But the dynamics have changed radically since the Darfur Peace Agreement was signed in May

2006, requiring the international community to reconstruct its strategy for peace from its very foundations.

Start from the basics: the Darfur Peace Agreement has failed. Whatever promise it held as a step towards ending violence and creating power-sharing structures when it was signed by the National Congress Party and a faction of the insurgent Sudan Liberation Army, has long since evaporated. There is no settlement, and the international community has struggled to unify its approach towards one. Meanwhile, the situation on the ground has been deteriorating.

In part because of the National Congress Party's divide-and-rule policies, rebel groups have splintered. After years of suffering brutal raids by government forces and their proxy militias, civilians are increasingly at risk from rebel groups, as are aid workers, African Union [a federation of African nations] peacekeepers and even internally displaced persons in the camps.

International peace efforts must align themselves with this new reality in Darfur.

Dissent is also growing among Darfur's Arab tribes, leading to new alliances with non-Arab groups, and sparking clashes between and within Arab tribes and Arab-led groups. Some simply want to secure their gains from the last few years of war, especially before the peacekeepers arrive.

Sudan's Arabs are also faced with a new choice: confront the incoming African Union-United Nations peacekeeping force and continue fighting a proxy war for the government, or distance themselves from the National Congress Party and engage with the international community.

More and more Darfurian Arabs feel betrayed by the party, whose strategy is based on a belief that the longer Darfur remains disunited and in disarray, the longer the party will stay in power. But Arab defections from the Khartoum-led fold have not brought about stable alliances or a coherent opposition, only a murkier picture and more chaos on the ground.

Peace Efforts in the New Reality

International peace efforts must align themselves with this new reality in Darfur. The only way to make progress is to give enough time for ongoing rebel unification efforts to succeed, and to broaden talks to involve the full range of actors in the conflict. On the latter, the AU-UN [African Union-United Nations] joint mediation team must return to Darfur for further consultations that bring in all constituencies on core issues such as land tenure, grazing rights, local administration and the cessation of hostilities.

The stakes are high. If we get it wrong this time, the chaos will accelerate . . . [into] a spreading civil war in Sudan.

They must seek to identify individuals to represent the interests of these groups at the peace talks, giving specific attention to the representation of women, civil society, the internally displaced and Arabs. Full participation can be achieved either by convening a Darfur-wide forum with representatives of all constituencies, or by expanding the consultations conducted earlier in 2007 through the existing, though moribund, Darfur-Darfur Dialogue and Consultation process.

Neighbouring countries need to be involved in the Darfur peace process. Chad and the Central African Republic receive thousands of refugees. Libya, Chad, Eritrea and Egypt, are all integral players with influence over various rebel movements and the National Congress Party. If any peace is to be negotiated, they need to be included in the mediation. The top priority in new negotiations should be a ceasefire agreement, incorporating all actors to the conflict.

Despite the urgency generated by ongoing bloodshed in Darfur, the international community must avoid the trap of thinking there are quick fixes. Indeed, too much haste to do a deal was a key reason the Darfur Peace Agreement failed to deliver.

The Libya peace negotiations are now [December 2007] in recess. The international community would be wise to use the delay to organise an effective and appropriate strategy for the months ahead. More generally, coordinated international focus must also be directed at supporting the implementation of Sudan's North-South peace agreement, which provides the constitutional basis for peace in Darfur and Sudan's democratisation process.

The stakes are high. If we get it wrong this time, the chaos will accelerate, and the AU-UN force arriving in Darfur will not only have no peace to keep but may even find itself surrounded by a spreading civil war in Sudan.

Divestment Campaigns Against China May Be the Most Effective Tool for Saving Darfur

Daniel Millenson

Daniel Millenson is a student at Brandeis University in Waltham, Massachusetts, and a national advocacy director and co-founder of the Sudan Divestment Task Force, a project of the Genocide Intervention Network.

When confronted by the crime of genocide, human rights activists do not typically dash to state capitols. Since 1787, foreign policy has remained outside states' bailiwick, with Congress and the President serving as more appropriate venues for foreign policymaking. So when the United States declared the atrocities unfolding in Sudan's vast Darfur region to constitute genocide in 2004, activists rightly responded by flooding Congressional mailboxes and crowding the Washington [DC] Mall, demanding an end to the violence.

Khartoum lies acutely vulnerable to economic pressure.

However, as subsequent failed cease-fires and watered-down UN [United Nations] resolutions demonstrated, too many vital economic interests were at stake to alter Darfur's bloody status quo. In an attempt to break the logjam, several student activists across the country began to follow the money, discovering that more than 70% of Sudan's oil revenues is steered towards the country's military expenditures, fueling the genocide in Darfur. Additionally, the mostly Asian oil companies operating in the country's petroleum sector have committed human rights abuses of their own, facilitated arms transfers, and in at least one case, refueled military aircraft. Because Sudan's foreign debt exceeds its gross domestic product, and the country possesses little capability for indigenous oil production, Khartoum [Sudan's capital and seat of government] lies acutely vulnerable to economic pressure. Although longstanding US sanctions mean that American companies are rarely involved with Sudan, university endowments and city/state pension funds are investing in the very firms that are underpinning the regime.

Harvard University became the first institution to divest from Sudan.

The Beginning: Students and Campuses

In April 2005, Harvard University became the first institution to divest from Sudan, shedding holdings in Chinese oil company PetroChina. Although a smattering of colleges and states followed Harvard's lead, their approaches differed significantly, including anywhere from one to more than 150 companies for divestment in their sundry policies.

As a student urging my own school, Brandeis University, to divest, I sought to organize the inchoate movement, cofounding the Sudan Divestment Task Force with University of California [UC] divestment leaders Jason Miller and Adam Sterling. In the process of pushing the UC Regents to divest, Jason had developed a model of divestment known as "targeted divestment," which surgically focuses only on companies that substantially aid the government, do not benefit civilians outside the government, have refused to take even minimal steps (such as pressuring the government to change its behavior) to ameliorate the situation in Darfur, and have proven unresponsive to shareholder engagement on the issue.

The resultant 2–3 dozen "highest offending" firms turn out to be clustered in (surprise!) Sudan's problematic petroleum sector.

The targeted model stood in stark contrast to the "blanket" approach of the Apartheid South Africa divestment campaign, which included more than one-third of the S&P 500 [a list of 500 commonly traded stocks in the United States]. Although effective in helping to end apartheid [in 1990], the campaign's broad sweep exacerbated a paucity of infrastructure development and foreign direct investment that disproportionately hurt the poor—not to mention crimped portfolio returns for divesting institutions. With its careful differentiation between good and bad corporate actors, the targeted divestment model quickly gained currency with both humanitarians and fiduciaries [institutions that invest money], starting with the University of California, which adopted the policy in March 2006.

Divestment's market mechanism is as simple as supply and demand—reduce demand for a given stock and as long as supply remains constant, share price will drop.

Bigger Fish: Public Pension Funds

Divestment's market mechanism is as simple as supply and demand—reduce demand for a given stock and as long as supply remains constant, share price will drop. Should share price fall enough, aggrieved shareholders and shrinking executive stock options force the firm to change tack. In the case of Sudan, such a change would entail improving corporate behavior or leaving the country entirely, thus depriving Khartoum of the funds it needs to perpetrate genocide. Although schools like Harvard and the UC maintain multi-billion dollar endowments, those sizeable sums nevertheless make universities mere minnows in the ocean of institutional investing. In order to successfully dent highest offenders' share prices, we needed to net bigger fish. We found them in the form of US city and state public employee pension funds, which, in the aggregate, total in the trillions of dollars.

Following that imperative, we began to move from college campuses to state capitols. Needless to say, the transition necessitated a new scale of organizing, as well as increased outreach to community and faith-based groups. In California, those foundations were already laid during the UC campaign. After months of hearings, votes, and nail-biting, Governor Arnold Schwarzenegger signed the nation's first targeted divestment bill in September 2006, [and] with the stroke of a pen, Schwarzenegger ensured that more than $400 billion worth of pension fund assets would not indirectly finance genocide. When most other state legislatures reconvened in January [2007], a trickle of state divestment laws rapidly turned into a flood. Like Congress, constituents can call and write their state legislators to voice concerns on an issue. Unlike Congress, state legislators often respond. At present time, twenty states have divested, including the likes of Texas, New York, and Florida.

Signs of Success

As a growing number of states have passed divestment legislation, companies previously unresponsive to more than two years of shareholder engagement suddenly perked up, anxious to move off the highest offenders list. Several major firms operating in Sudan did just that, either by changing problematic behavior or leaving the country entirely. High-profile divestment-induced departures have included Rolls Royce, previously making engines for a China National Petroleum Corporation/PetroChina oil block in South Darfur. In the words of one expert, "divestment campaigns may prove more effective than sanctions."

Just as noteworthy, the Sudanese government has been correspondingly shrill, condemning divestment at every opportunity. Last year saw the regime place an eight-page, million-dollar ad in the *New York Times* to counteract the movement.

Divestment remains activists' sharpest tool for changing Khartoum's genocidal calculus.

Perhaps most significant has been China's response. By far the largest player in Sudan's oil industry, crude-thirsty China was long content to stay mum on Darfur. However, divestment's focus on the Sino-Sudanese arms-oil relationship has since broken China's silence. Galled by Western outcry, China has appointed a special envoy for Darfur, sent senior officials to visit refugee camps, and nudged Sudan into accepting UN peacekeepers. Such actions stand out even more starkly considering the country's traditional unwillingness, for obvious reasons, to criticize the human rights records of other sovereign states. Although China remains a roadblock to more robust UN action, it nevertheless appears to be taking its first, halting steps towards a more constructive approach in Darfur.

Now, in the wake of its US successes, the divestment movement is spreading to Canada and Europe. Additionally, asset managers with large holdings in highest offenders are increasingly moving into the movement's crosshairs, with a nascent shareholder campaign pressing them to utilize their leverage and rigorously engage these firms. Companies are now more inclined to ask, "What can we do to get off your list?" than to give concerned shareholders the cold shoulder. With diplomatic and military solutions still lethally slow, divestment remains activists' sharpest tool for changing Khartoum's genocidal calculus.

China Is Not the Answer to the Darfur Crisis

Morton Abramowitz and Jonathan Kolieb

Morton Abramowitz is a senior fellow at the Century Foundation and a former president of the Carnegie Endowment for International Peace—both nonprofit public policy organizations. Jonathan Kolieb is a research associate at the Century Foundation.

After four years of tireless efforts, Darfur advocacy groups have had little success in pressuring the [George W.] Bush administration or any other Western government to move decisively against the Sudanese government for its atrocities in Darfur. These groups are right to dismiss the Bush administration's latest sanctions initiative as mere posturing; like all of the president's efforts to date, it's too limited in scope and lacks a wider, more holistic diplomatic strategy. These groups are focusing instead on the two C's of humanitarian advocacy—China and celebrities—as a remedy for a crisis that has killed over 200,000 people and displaced more than 2.5 million. But in pointing the finger at China, proponents of stronger action on Darfur are merely helping the White House evade moral responsibility for a humanitarian disaster that it labels a "genocide."

China is a convenient whipping boy, and a cast of celebrities has signed on eagerly to lead the whipping.

Blaming China

With its oil ties to the Sudanese regime and its resistance to U.N. [United Nations] Security Council [the main decision-making body of the United Nations] resolutions condemning

Morton Abramowitz and Jonathan Kolieb, "Why China Won't Save Darfur," *Foreign Policy*, June 2007. Reproduced by permission.

Khartoum [Sudan's capital and seat of government], China is a convenient whipping boy, and a cast of celebrities has signed on eagerly to lead the whipping. Hollywood heavyweights Steven Spielberg, Mia Farrow, and George Clooney have come out in recent weeks to criticize the Chinese government for not responding to the cries of Darfur's people, zeroing in on the 2008 Beijing Olympics. Earnest editorial writers have joined them enthusiastically.

The campaign has had some results. Beijing's usual foreign policy approach—"non-interference" in Sudan's domestic affairs—has been evolving under the pressure. China has become more active in trying to persuade the Khartoum regime to cooperate with the international community. China is willing to pursue a peace settlement, and indeed [Chinese] President Hu Jintao pressured Sudanese President Omar Hassan al-Bashir on this issue and duly urged cooperation with the United Nations on his visit to Khartoum in February [2007]. Beijing has also appointed a full-time envoy tasked with assisting in resolving the Darfur crisis.

Only a top-level, sustained, and aggressive multilateral mediation effort . . . can stop the violence and reverse the massive displacement of people.

Threats to China Will Not Save Darfur

But threatening a "Genocide Olympics" alone will not bring peace (or peacekeepers) to that troubled region. No amount of criticism will convince Beijing to pursue a coercive strategy and a nonconsensual deployment of U.N. peacekeepers that Khartoum rejects. Yes, China has the economic leverage to gain the ear of President Bashir, but that hardly means it has the ability—or, more to the point, the will—to bully him into accepting a large U.N. peacekeeping contingent in Darfur. China's multibillion dollar investments in Sudan's petroleum industry are a much-needed source of energy for its mush-rooming economy. Beijing may make tactical moves to pressure Sudan, but it will not choose human rights over oil, a matter of paramount national interest.

And, even if China were capable of delivering Bashir, the Sudanese government is not the only impediment to an effective peace process. Nowadays, more people may well be dying from tribal clashes than from marauding *janjaweed* [militia group] or government forces. The infighting of fractured rebel groups and the sheer number of displaced people with no homes to return to are also immediate and significant obstacles to peace. But China has little influence over the rebel movements and is ill-positioned to act as a mediator between them.

China is not going to do what the United States and Europe have been unwilling to do for the past four years.

Nor is China a good choice to be our moral compass. The West embraces human rights and international humanitarian law, but China emphatically does not. The continuing crisis not only threatens the lives of millions, but the weak Western response undermines those grandiose principles such as the "responsibility to protect"—hallmarks of our international moral code. Moreover, it is the U.S. government, not Beijing (nor the U.N., for that matter), that has invoked the label "genocide" to describe the Darfur crisis. Morally and legally, the responsibility to lead is America's.

Ending the Darfur conflict requires much more than what China alone can offer. Rhetorical flourishes from world leaders, limited Western unilateral sanctions, and promises of firmer action at some indeterminate time in the future are also patently insufficient. Only a top-level, sustained, and aggressive multilateral mediation effort backed by the United

States, the European Union, and African, Arab, and Chinese governments can stop the violence and reverse the massive displacement of people.

Advocacy groups deserve praise for bringing Darfur into the world's collective consciousness and generating funds to care for millions of dislocated civilians. But their latest campaign lets the U.S. and others off the hook. Highlighting China's woeful human rights record is important, but does little to resolve the conflict in Darfur. China is not going to do what the United States and Europe have been unwilling to do for the past four years.

The ICC's Indictment of Sudan's President Is the Right Thing for Darfur

Sara Darehshori

Sara Darehshori is senior counsel for Human Rights Watch's International Justice Program, which works to promote justice and accountability for genocide, war crimes, and crimes against humanity in countries where national courts are unable or unwilling to do so.

"When will Bashir be tried?" Darfurian refugees on the Chad border asked me time and again last summer [2007]. "We are here because of Bashir," they said.

Last July [2007], I went to Chad to look into how the International Criminal Court [ICC], which has a field office in [Chad city] Abeche and works with refugees in the camps, is performing on the ground. As part of my assessment, I interviewed dozens of refugees.

Considering the hardships the refugees faced daily, I was not sure how they would feel talking about a topic as abstract as accountability in an international forum.

Thus I was surprised when their reactions to my questions were positive, with even a hint of impatience because the ICC prosecutor had not yet gone after the president of Sudan, Omar Hassan Ahmed Bashir. A Sudanese official and a rebel leader had been indicted by The Hague-based court but, to the refugees, that didn't go far enough. The chain of command was clear.

On [July 11, 2008], Luis Moreno-Ocampo, the ICC chief prosecutor, sought a warrant from the court for the arrest of

Sara Darehshori, "Doing the Right Thing for Darfur: An ICC Indictment of Sudan's President Serves Peace and Justice," *Los Angeles Times*, July 15, 2008. Reproduced by permission of the author.

Bashir on charges of genocide, crimes against humanity and war crimes. It may take months for the court to rule, but Moreno-Ocampo's actions will, no doubt, be greeted with joy in the camps.

Some commentators outside Darfur have argued that . . . the prosecution of top officials . . . will interfere with prospects for peace and security.

A Lack of Accountability

Yet some commentators outside Darfur have argued that this "moment of jubilation" can only be a symbolic victory for the long-suffering people of that region. They contend that should the prosecution of top officials—however terrible their crimes—go forward, it will interfere with prospects for peace and security.

Sudan's history makes a strong case for the opposite conclusion: The persistent lack of accountability has instead undermined the prospects for peace and stability. There has been little peace to keep.

Most of the international attempts to persuade Khartoum to end the violence in Darfur have resulted in little cooperation.

Since taking power in a military coup in 1989, the leadership of the ruling party in Sudan has conducted brutal campaigns to combat rebel groups in several regions, forcibly displacing millions of Sudanese and killing up to 2 million people in southern Sudan alone, all with impunity.

The strategy of burning and looting villages and arming tribal militias to kill and steal from ethnic groups deemed supportive of rebels was initiated in the south, and for years, much of the international community stood by silently. Not one U.N. [United Nations] Security Council [the main decision-making body of the United Nations] resolution condemned the attacks throughout the 1990s.

International negotiators, understandably anxious to secure peace, were silent on the issue of accountability for fear of its effect on the peace talks; perpetrators of the most serious crimes were never held to account. When the Darfur insurgency began in 2003—during negotiations between the north and south—the Sudanese government returned to the same old tactics, committing widespread attacks on civilians in Darfur.

Today, it remains true that most of the international attempts to persuade Khartoum [Sudan's capital and seat of government] to end the violence in Darfur have resulted in little cooperation. In particular, relative silence on accountability and justice issues in Sudan has yielded extremely limited concessions from Sudan.

The government of Sudan remains obligated under international law to ensure the full, safe and unhindered access of relief personnel to all those in need in Darfur.

The Need to Support the ICC

When the ICC issued the first two warrants against suspects in Darfur, the Security Council did not speak out against Khartoum's blatant refusal to carry out the warrants. (Not only did Khartoum refuse to turn over those who were indicted, but one was promoted within the government.) Apparently the Security Council hoped that downplaying justice would help in the deployment of peacekeeping forces or compliance with the peace agreement. However, despite a resolution authorizing a U.N. peacekeeping force in Darfur, Khartoum continues to obstruct full deployment. Few bases have been established, and the forces are at barely a third of their authorized capacity.

Now there is concern that a Bashir warrant from the ICC will in particular threaten humanitarian efforts in Darfur. [In July 2008], seven U.N. peacekeepers were killed by attackers whose identities are still uncertain.

But with or without the Bashir warrant, the government of Sudan remains obligated under international law to ensure the full, safe and unhindered access of relief personnel to all those in need in Darfur. Attacks against personnel involved in a humanitarian or peacekeeping mission constitute war crimes. It is up to the Security Council to take measures, such as targeted sanctions, to ensure that Sudan abides by its obligations under international law.

In June [2008], the Security Council issued a unanimous statement calling for Sudan to cooperate with the ICC. That reaffirmed the council's historic commitment to bring justice to victims in Darfur. The international community should now stand with the ICC as it considers warrants against Bashir, which is a further step toward meaningful accountability for the massive crimes in the region.

As one Darfur refugee put it to me, "There is no justice in Sudan. If there was, we would not be here."

Regime Change Is the Only Way to Achieve Lasting Peace in Darfur

Nathaniel Myers

Nathaniel Myers is a political analyst who recently returned from Sudan.

[The January 2008] revelation that Sudan had appointed a notorious *janjaweed* militia leader to a senior government post was, as [the international advocacy group] Human Rights Watch rightly called it, "a stunning affront to victims" of the violence in Darfur.

It was not, however, much of a surprise. After all, Sudan's government already includes a state minister for humanitarian affairs who is one of just two men currently under indictment by the International Criminal Court for crimes in Darfur.

President Omar al-Bashir and his National Congress Party (NCP) have long demonstrated their contempt for both Darfur and international opinion.

No, President Omar al-Bashir and his National Congress Party (NCP) have long demonstrated their contempt for both Darfur and international opinion, to the enormous detriment of the new United Nations peacekeeping mission, which remains undermanned, undersupplied, and undermined. Last month, a coalition of prominent nongovernmental organizations accurately described it as being "set up to fail."

The Need for Regime Change

The United States and its allies on Darfur have long responded to [Sudan's capital city] Khartoum's obstructions with public

Nathaniel Myers, "Darfur's Best Hope: The Ballot Box: A Regime-Ousting Election Could Help More Than Peacekeepers," *Christian Science Monitor*, January 25, 2008. Reproduced by permission of the author.

complaints and reaffirmations of their commitment to the mission. Though well-intentioned, this approach has played into the NCP's hands. While American attention has been narrowly focused on the struggling peacekeeping mission, the NCP has been undercutting a potentially dramatic challenge to its rule—and with it, the greatest opportunity for lasting peace in Darfur. With the swearing in [January 2008] of a new special envoy for Sudan, Rich Williamson, it is time that America revisits its approach to Sudan—and recognizes that the peacekeeping mission should not be its exclusive focus.

As Mr. Bashir's latest provocation suggests, the problem in Darfur is one that ultimately cannot be resolved by peace-keepers. That's because its roots don't lie in local grievances or ethnic divisions—though both have fueled the fighting—but in the halls of power in Khartoum. The peacekeeping mission is urgently needed to improve immediate security, but lasting peace will come to Darfur and the rest of Sudan only when the country is led by a government genuinely committed to the cause. Remove the NCP from power and, as a senior UN [United Nations] official in Sudan told me recently, "the problem in Darfur is over."

A Chance of Revolution

In most misgoverned nations, talk of such regime change would seem little more than a pipe dream—but remarkably, improbably, there exists in Sudan today a chance of revolution through the ballot box. Under the terms of an existing but neglected peace agreement, signed in 2005 to end the 21-year civil war between the Khartoum government and southern rebels, Sudan is obligated to hold a national election by July 2009. This peace deal, known as the Comprehensive Peace Agreement (CPA), also promised the south a referendum on independence in 2011. Next year's [2009] election is essentially the last chance to stave off what will otherwise be a resounding vote for southern secession, by showing southerners that they will be allowed to compete for national power in a unified, democratic Sudan.

Of course, commitments from Khartoum are always suspect, and there is particular reason to expect the NCP to break this one. Since seizing power in 1989, the NCP has attacked, marginalized, or alienated too much of the electorate to win fairly. It is widely expected to do all it can to delay, manipulate, and potentially even cancel the vote. Two years past deadline, the national parliament has yet to pass an election bill, while the NCP spent much of 2007 stalling on its commitments under the CPA, which included several critical election precursors.

If the US wants to see long-term peace in Sudan, the new special envoy must place greater emphasis on . . . the conduct of a free, fair, and potentially regime-shattering election.

With foreign attention concentrated so intensely on the peacekeeping mission, these failures have provoked only minimal international protest. To mark the third anniversary of the CPA earlier this month, for instance, the White House released a statement of just two paragraphs—one of which was a reiteration of Washington's [that is, the United States'] commitment to the peacekeeping mission.

This represents a tragically shortsighted approach to Sudan; the elections deserve to be much more than just an afterthought for American diplomats. To be sure, it is hard to be optimistic that Bashir will ever permit an election that threatens his grip on power. But any vote, however flawed, will challenge the entrenched political order and give the opposition a chance to organize. Its conduct also represents the only scenario through which Sudan might survive as a unified state past the south's likely secession vote in 2011. And despite provocations such as this latest appointment, recent history shows that even the NCP can be influenced by a sustained campaign of targeted international pressure: Recall its eventual acquiescence to the UN peacekeeping mission.

With its current focus on peacekeepers, the [George W.] Bush administration risks allowing this critical election to become just another broken NCP promise. The peacekeeping mission in Darfur is surely important, but if the US wants to see long-term peace in Sudan, the new special envoy must place greater emphasis on the implementation of the CPA and the conduct of a free, fair, and potentially regime-shattering election.

Darfur's Crisis Requires a Solution from Islam

Hizb ut-Tahrir

Hizb ut-Tahrir is a global Islamic political party established in 1953 to bring the Muslims back to living an Islamic way of life under the rule of Islamic governments.

The situation in Darfur, Sudan, has drawn much attention.... For an African country it has surprisingly received much widespread coverage in the Western media. Significantly it has been the focus of attention for many western politicians, particularly [US president] George Bush and [former British Prime Minister] Tony Blair, a focus perhaps only second to Iraq when it comes to foreign affairs.

The fact that leaders such as Tony Blair and George Bush are raising apparent concern for Darfur and its people is enough to raise suspicions in itself. The rather simplistic view presented by the Western media has been one of the Sudanese regime arming 'Arab' militias, the Janjaweed, to attack the native 'Black African' population in Darfur. The US regime has gone as far as calling the actions 'genocide' on the part of the Sudanese regime. However, after witnessing the aggressive, violent and illegitimate occupations of Iraq and Afghanistan it is only right that one examine the situation in Darfur very closely rather than taking these statements at face value.

The Situation in Darfur

Certainly it is true that fighting is and has been taking place in Darfur. In fact many aid agencies estimate that hundreds of thousands may have been killed, with estimates varying from 50,000 up to half a million, with 200,000 being the most likely figure. Another 2.5 million people have been displaced from their homes as refugees. Yet much of the Western media and international community have chosen to ignore many of the facts surrounding this conflict in yet another strategically positioned Muslim country in the world.

It is important to recognise that the Sudanese regime, Janjaweed or Arab militia and the rebels in Darfur are all Muslims. The Janjaweed are drawn from the Baggra . . . tribes, mainly Bedouin herders whilst the rebels come from the Fur, Zaghawa and Massaleit tribes, mainly land tillers. The Sudanese regime has been fighting several rebel groups drawn from these tribes opposed to its rule. The conflict started in 2003 when a rebel group started attacking Sudanese regime targets after accusing Khartoum [Sudan's capital city and seat of government] of neglecting the area. There are two main rebel groups, the Sudan Liberation Army (SLA) and the Justice and Equality Movement (JEM). The conflict has also spilled over into Chad, which is fighting its own civil war with both the Sudanese and Chad regimes accusing each other of supporting their respective opposing rebel forces.

The Darfur rebels themselves have internal differences. The SLA and the JEM have merged into the National Redemption Front led by a former Darfur governor after the SLA split, with the larger faction led by Minni Minnawi agreeing to the Darfur Peace Agreement (DPA) with the Sudanese regime in May 2006. Unlike the civil war in Sudan, which was fought by the primarily Muslim north against the minority Christian south, all parties in this conflict are Muslim. Thus the presentation of the conflict as one of 'Arabs' against 'Africans' is not accurate and is deliberately misleading. All of the people are black African, indigenous and Muslim. Sudan is a country of more than 40 million people, 70% of whom are Muslim, made up of more than 80 different ethnic groups and tribes, speaking many different languages including Arabic. Of these, nearly 8 million live in Darfur, an area the size of France.

Studying Sudan's past history gives an understanding as to the basis of Darfur and the whole of Sudan's current problems. Sudan is a country that only achieved independence from British rule in 1956. Prior to that it was captured by a proxy Anglo-Egyptian force in 1899 following the defeat of the Mahdist forces, with Egypt itself being part of the British Empire at that time.[1] Darfur itself was actually captured by the British in 1916, after which financial support from Khartoum for the outer regions such as Darfur ebbed away creating wealth inequalities in Sudan as a whole.

The British implemented a number of polices to ensure their continued colonial rule. They divided Sudan into north and south, developing the north whilst isolating the south from northern Sudan. They prevented people from the north entering the south. They actively discouraged the spread of Islam, the practice of Islamic customs and introduced Christian missionaries and sought to reintroduce what they called the indigenous 'African' identity. Most important of all during the 1920s and 1930s the British sought to rule indirectly by strengthening pliant village sheikhs in the north and tribal leaders in the south, helping to create a fractured and weak ruling system in Sudan.

As in other similar conflicts, poverty is one of the issues fuelling the current conflict today, compounded by nationalistic and tribal rivalries between the people in Darfur. After its independence Sudan struggled with its first civil war before in the 1970s it overcame this and adopted policies more independent from the West. However peace was not permanent and in 1983 the civil war in Sudan restarted which eventually came to an end again in 2003. The Americans supported the Christian rebels during this conflict. No sooner had a peace agreement been agreed to end the second civil war, the Darfur conflict had started. Sudan's short history of sovereignty has

1. The Madhist Revolt was led by Muhammad Ahmad, also called the "Madhi." It liberated Sudan from Ottoman rule.

seen little peace with outside forces playing a major part in helping to destabilise a resource-rich and strategically important country.

The Role of Oil

The other point of fact that is not widely reported is that Darfur is rich with oil, as is the rest of southern Sudan. The oil from Darfur accounts for $4 billion of revenue for the Sudanese regime, over half of the regime's income. Most importantly the current Sudanese regime has close ties with China, which has strong oil interests in Darfur, with Sudan supplying up to 10% of China's oil imports. America has oil interests in neighbouring Chad but has been shut out of Sudan.

It is remarkable that . . . issues such as oil and rivalry between powers such as China and America are largely overlooked in the international Western media.

It is remarkable that despite apparent concerns for the people of Darfur, issues such as oil and rivalry between powers such as China and America are largely overlooked in the international Western media. Indeed towards the south in neighbouring Uganda there is also internal strife, led by the Christian Lord's Resistance Army, where similar ethnic killings are taking place, with rebels operating from southern Sudan, yet very few people would even be aware of this. As with other developing countries, countries such as Sudan are vulnerable to external forces that covertly exploit local problems and help foster opposition to the central regime depending upon their particular interest. Little wonder then that the Darfur rebels seem surprisingly well armed and funded. If America chose to launch an illegal war and invasion of oil rich Iraq, how can one reasonably expect America not to be motivated by the same in Darfur again?

This is why calls for outside intervention by Western powers need to be viewed in this context. The UN [United Nations] resolution 1706 passed in August 2006 calling for the deployment of up to 20,000 UN peacekeepers—to replace the current 7000 African Union [a federation of African nations] force—only creates an avenue for foreign intervention in Sudan as a first step towards loosening control over Darfur from the Sudanese regime. As with other Muslim lands, this is another opportunity for colonialists to gain a foothold in this resource-rich land by seeking to somehow legitimise their intervention under the guise of the UN, which is simply nothing more than a tool for predatory colonial powers that are locked in their never ending rivalry for resources. In this case if America cannot gain access to the oil, than at the very least it will seek to deny China being able to access oil in the region by helping to create and perpetuate the conflict.

Often portrayed in the Western media is that Sudan's regime is 'Islamic'. This is not true.

Islam Is the Real Solution

The other assertion often portrayed in the Western media is that Sudan's regime is 'Islamic'. This is not true. Like all other Muslim countries it implements some aspects of Shari'ah [Islamic law] along side many other non-Islamic laws and does not fulfill the conditions of a true Islamic State which can only be on the method of Allah's messenger (saw), the Khilafah [or Caliphate: Muslim political leadership]. Moreover the spilling of innocent Muslim blood such as that in Darfur, in which the regime has clearly played a role, is not permitted and is a severe crime under the Shari'ah and the Sudanese regime is a transgressor like many other regimes plaguing the Muslim world today. Sudan's regime is oppressive towards its own people having illegitimately seized power. It came to power via a military coup prolonged by the facade of rigged elections, whilst being courted by outside nations such as China, who have their own interests at heart and continue to provide diplomatic and military support. Just recently China agreed to increase military support.

By looking further back at Sudan's history one can see the inspiration for a real solution to the problems at hand. Islam was introduced into North Africa hundreds of years ago, with Islam entering much of the Darfur region as well as other parts of Sudan in the 14th century. Most of the Muslim rulers modelled their ruling on the Khilafah, although the Funj Sultanate of Sinnar [north Sudan] was not directly under the control of the Uthmani Khilafah at the time until 1821. Yet this still brought together people irrespective of ethnicity and prosperity ensued. This is because the people put aside their petty rivalries and were united on the basis of Islam.

The only way out of Sudan's internal fighting is to unify the people around Islam leaving aside all ethnic and tribal affinities.

Today the only way out of Sudan's internal fighting is to unify the people around Islam leaving aside all ethnic and tribal affinities, which can only come with the proper implementation of Islam. Only the establishment of the Khilafah in the Muslim lands will remove corrupt regimes such as the Sudanese regime and safeguard the Muslims in Sudan from greedy colonial powers. It will look after the affairs of all the Muslims not only in Darfur but in the rest of Sudan and beyond and help heal ethnic divisions between the many different tribes. We know that Islam took the divided Arabs during the time of the Messenger of Allah (saw) from a pathetic divided lot to a position of great power as Islam ruled from the west coast of Africa to the Indus Valley in the Indian subcontinent within 100 years under the Khilafah. As Sudan's history shows, any externally enforced solutions can only serve predatory colonial powers at the expense of the Muslims in Darfur. Once again it is being proven that because of the weakness of the Muslims, because of the absence of the Khilafah, Muslim blood is now also being spilt with impunity in Sudan as well.

Organizations to Contact

The editors have compiled the following list of organizations concerned with the issues debated in this book. The descriptions are derived from materials provided by the organizations. All have publications or information available for interested readers. The list was compiled on the date of publication of the present volume; names, addresses, and phone numbers may change. Be aware that many organizations take several weeks or longer to respond to inquiries, so allow as much time as possible.

Amnesty International USA
5 Penn Plaza, New York, NY 10001
(212) 807-8400 • fax: (212) 627-1451
e-mail: aimember@aiusa.org
Web site: www.aiusa.org

Amnesty International is a grassroots activist organization with over 1.8 million members worldwide; Amnesty International USA (AIUSA) is the U.S. section. The organization's mission is to prevent and end abuses of human rights, including the rights to physical and mental integrity, freedom of conscience and expression, and freedom from discrimination. The group's Web site features a section on Darfur with news, photos, fact sheets, background information, and reports such as "Displaced in Darfur: A Generation of Anger" and "Time Is Not on Our Side: An Agenda for the Darfur Peacekeeping Mission."

Darfur Peace & Development Organization
666 11th St. NW, Suite 315, Washington, DC 20001
(202) 393-8150 • fax: (202) 393-8151
e-mail: info@darfurpeace.org
Web site: www.darfurpeace.org

Darfur Peace & Development Organization (DPDO) is a non-profit, nongovernmental organization founded in 2002 by a group of Darfurians in the United States. DPDO's mission is to provide humanitarian relief to victims of the genocide in Darfur, to facilitate just governance, and to enable Darfurians to rebuild and develop their homeland. The DPDO Web site includes numerous reports on Darfur and Sudan, such as "Sudan Survivors Answer Your Questions" and "Sudan's Children at a Crossroads: An Urgent Need for Protection."

The ENOUGH Project
1225 Eye St. NW, Suite 307, Washington, DC   20005
(202) 682-1611 • fax: (202) 682-6140
Web site: www.enoughproject.org

ENOUGH is a project of the Center for American Progress, a liberal think tank, which works to propose viable policy recommendations and help build a permanent consitutency to prevent genocide and crimes against humanity around the world. The group focuses on the situations in Congo, northern Uganda, Darfur, southern Sudan, and the spillover violence in Chad. The ENOUGH Web site features reports on the crisis in Darfur such as "Irresolution: The U.N. Security Council on Darfur" and "Sudanese President Omar al-Bashir: The Record Speaks for Itself."

Human Rights First
333 Seventh Ave., 13th Floor, New York, NY   10001-5108
(212) 845-5200 • fax: (212) 845-5299
e-mail: feedback@humanrightsfirst.org
Web site: www.humanrightsfirst.org

Human Rights First (HRF) was founded in 1978 as the Lawyers Committee for International Human Rights to promote laws and policies that advance universal rights and freedoms. The organization's mission is to protect people at risk, including refugees, victims of torture or other mass human rights violations, and victims of discrimination. It accomplishes this mission by advocating for changes in government and international policies, seeking justice through the courts, and raising awareness and understanding through the media. The

Web site has links to background information about Darfur, policy papers on various issues related to the conflict, as well as HRF campaign alerts.

Human Rights Watch
1630 Connecticut Ave. NW, Suite 500
Washington, DC   20009
(202) 612-4321 • fax: (202) 612-4333
e-mail: hrwdc@hrw.org
Web site: www.hrw.org

Human Rights Watch (HRW) is an independent, nongovernmental organization, supported by contributions from private individuals and foundations worldwide. HRW conducts fact-finding investigations into human rights abuses, and publishes those findings in books and reports. HRW also meets with government officials to urge changes in policy and practice and provides up-to-the-minute information about conflicts that are are underway. The organization's Web site contains a section on Darfur with maps, background information, recent news, and numerous reports such as "Darfur 2007: Chaos by Design," "Ensuring Civilian Protection in Chad," and "Darfur: Humanitarian Aid Under Siege."

International Crisis Group
1629 K St. NW, Suite 450, Washington, DC   20006
(202) 785-1601 • fax: (202) 785-1630
Web site: www.crisisgroup.org

The International Crisis Group (ICG) is an independent, non-profit, nongovernmental organization that works on five continents, conducting field-based research and high-level advocacy to prevent and resolve deadly conflict. Darfur is one of the ICG's major concerns and its Web site contains a section on Sudan that includes background information on the country, a special analysis titled "Crisis in Darfur," as well as links to articles, reports, and news items on the Darfur conflict.

Physicians for Human Rights
2 Arrow St., Suite 301, Cambridge, MA   02138
(617) 301-4200 • fax: (617) 301-4250
Web site: http://physiciansforhumanrights.org

Physicians for Human Rights (PHR) mobilizes health professionals to advance health, dignity, justice, and the right to
health for all. PHR investigates human rights abuses and works
to stop them. The group publishes reports such as "Darfur:
Assault on Survival," "The Use of Rape as a Weapon of War in
the Conflict in Darfur, Sudan," and "Darfur Destroyed."

Save Darfur Coalition
2120 L St. NW, Suite 335, Washington, DC   20037
(800) 917-2034 • fax: (202) 478-6312
e-mail: info@savedarfur.org
Web site: www.savedarfur.org

The Save Darfur Coalition is an alliance of over 100 faith-
based, humanitarian and human rights organizations committed to raising awareness about the Darfur violence and working to help the people of the Darfur region. Its Web site offers
information about pending and passed legislation, as well as
policy and background papers on Darfur. Examples include
"Charged with Genocide: Implications of the ICC's case
Against Sudanese President al-Bashir" and "Darfur Update—
June 2008."

24 Hours for Darfur
260 Fifth Ave., 9th Floor, New York, NY   10001
e-mail: info@24hoursfordarfur.org
Web site: www.24hoursfordarfur.org

24 Hours for Darfur, a project of the nonprofit organization
Res Publica, Inc., is a global video advocacy campaign dedi-
cated to ending the conflict in Darfur and promoting peace
and security for the people living there. The campaign uses
digital video and online media to strengthen Darfur advocacy
and make it more direct, participatory, and global. Visitors to

the Web site can watch expert videos, testimony from Darfurians, and appeals for help from people around the world, and can e-mail messages about Darfur to political representatives and world leaders.

United Nations Office of the High Commissioner for Human Rights (OHCHR)

Palais Wilson, 52 rue des Pâquis, Geneva   CH-1201
  Switzerland
+41 22 917 90 00
e-mail: InfoDesk@ohchr.org
Web site: www.ohchr.org

The mission of OHCHR is to work for the protection of all human rights for all people, to help people realize their rights, and to assist those responsible for upholding such rights to ensure that they are implemented. To carry out this mission, the OHCHR works with governments, legislatures, courts, national institutions, civil society, and regional and international organizations. The OHCHR Web site has links to press releases, reports, and news items on Darfur.

U.S. Agency for International Development (USAID)

Ronald Reagan Building, Washington, DC   20523-1000
(202) 712-4320 • fax: (202) 216-3524
Web site: www.usaid.gov

USAID is the principal U.S. federal agency that extends assistance to countries recovering from disaster, trying to escape poverty, and engaging in democratic reforms. USAID promotes long-term and equitable economic growth, trade, health, democracy, conflict prevention, and humanitarian assistance in countries around the world. Its Web site contains a section on sub-Saharan Africa and a wealth of information on Sudan and the humanitarian crisis in Darfur.

Bibliography

Books

Agnes van
Ardenne-van der
Hoeven et al.

*Explaining Darfur: Lectures on the
Ongoing Genocide.* Amsterdam:
Amsterdam University Press, 2007.

J. Millard Burr
and Robert O.
Collins

Darfur: The Long Road to Disaster.
Princeton, NJ: Markus Wiener
Publishers, 2008.

Don Cheadle and
John Prendergast

*Not on Our Watch: The Mission to
End Genocide in Darfur and Beyond.*
Redwood Shores, CA: Hyperion,
2007.

M.W. Daly

*Darfur's Sorrow: A History of
Destruction and Genocide.* New York:
Cambridge University Press, 2007.

Julie Flint et al.

*War in Darfur and the Search for
Peace.* Boston, MA: Global Equity
Initiative, Harvard University, 2007.

John Hagan
and Wenona
Rymond-
Richmond

Darfur and the Crime of Genocide.
New York: Cambridge University
Press, 2008.

Daoud Hari

*The Translator: A Tribesman's Memoir
of Darfur.* New York: Random House,
2008.

Leora Kahn
and Jon Alter

*Darfur: Twenty Years of War and
Genocide in Sudan.* Brooklyn, NY:
PowerHouse Books, 2008.

Melissa
Leembruggen

The Sudan Project: Rebuilding with the People of Darfur—A Young Person's Guide. Nashville, TN: Abingdon Press, 2007.

Mahmood
Mamdani

Saviors and Survivors: Darfur, Politics, and the War on Terror. New York: Pantheon, 2009.

Jen Marlowe
et al.

Darfur Diaries: Stories of Survival. New York: Nation Books, 2006.

Samantha Power
et al.

Darfur Darfur. New York: DK Melcher Media, 2008.

Gerard Prunier

Darfur: The Ambiguous Genocide. Ithaca, NY: Cornell University Press, 2008.

Eric Reeves

A Long Day's Dying: Critical Moments in the Darfur Genocide. Toronto: Key Publishing House, 2007.

Brian Steidle
et al.

The Devil Came on Horseback: Bearing Witness to the Genocide in Darfur. New York: PublicAffairs, 2007.

Samuel Totten
and Eric
Markusen, eds.

Genocide in Darfur: Investigating the Atrocities in the Sudan. New York: Routledge, 2006.

Logan Williams,
ed.

We Hear You: American Kids' Reflections on Darfur. Reston, VA: Open Doors Publishing, 2007.

Periodicals

Jonathan Alter — "Boycott Opening Ceremonies," *Newsweek*, April 21, 2008.

America — "Darfur's Displaced People," March 3, 2008.

Hilary Andersson — "China 'Is Fuelling War in Darfur,'" *BBC News*, July 13, 2008. http://news.bbc.co.uk/2/hi/africa/7503428.stm.

BBC News — "AU Rejects Bashir Darfur Charges," July 21, 2008. http://news.bbc.co.uk/2/hi/africa/7517393.stm.

David Bosco — "'If We Die Today, You Will Be Responsible,'" *Spectator*, June 14, 2008.

CBS News — "Arab League Slams Sudan Genocide Charges," July 19, 2008. www.cbsnews.com/stories/2008/07/19/world/main4275553.shtml?source=RSSattr=World_4275553.

Thalif Deen — "UN Chief Urges Greater Level of Commitment to Darfur Mission," *Jane's Defence Weekly*, April 16, 2008.

Economist (US) — "Peacekeepers into the Fray: Sudan," March 13, 2008.

Moira Herbst — "Oil for China, Guns for Darfur," *Business Week Online*, March 14, 2008. www.businessweek.com/globalbiz/content/mar2008/gb20080314_430126.htm.

Catherine Holahan	"'Click Here to Save Darfur,'" *Business Week Online*, February 14, 2008. www.businessweek.com/technology/content/feb2008/tc20080213_617723.htm.
Human Rights Watch	"Darfur, No Redress for Rape: Five Years On, Sexual Violence Still Rife in Darfur," April 7, 2008. www.hrw.org/english/docs/2008/04/03/darfur18424.htm.
Charlayne Hunter-Gault	"A Crisis Up Close," *Essence*, March 2008.
Ted Johnson	"Games Over for Spielberg," *Daily Variety*, February 13, 2008.
Maclean's	"Dying in Darfur," January 14, 2008.
Normandy Madden	"China: West Is Overreacting," *Advertising Age*, March 31, 2008.
Elaine Monaghan and Liriel Higa	"Diplomatic Inertia Keeps Darfur Equation Bleak," *CQ Weekly*, February 18, 2008.
New Internationalist	"Darfur: A History," June 2007. www.newint.org/features/2007/06/01/history.
Daniel Pepper	"Chasing Darfur's Guns," *Mother Jones*, March–April 2008.
Lydia Polgreen	"Darfur's Agony: Does Even More Misery Lie Ahead for This Wartorn Region of Sudan?" *New York Times Upfront*, April 14, 2008.

Carina Ray   "Darfur and the Crisis of
                    Governance in Sudan," *New African*,
                    April 2008.

Tony Romm   "Carter Says Darfur Not Genocide,"
                    The Eagle, October 25, 2007.
                    http://media.www.theeagleonline.com/
                    media/storage/paper666/news/2007/
                    10/25/News/Carter.Says.Darfur.Not.
                    Genocide-3055112.shtml.

Patricia Treble   "Africa Casts a Shadow on the
                    Olympics," *Maclean's*, March 3, 2008.

Darrell Turner   "The Ingredients of Genocide,"
                    National Catholic Reporter, April 4,
                    2008.

Index